Mastering
Wing Chun
Kung Fu

Mastering Wing Chun Kung Fu

Samuel Kwok & Tony Massengill

EMPIRE Books

P.O. Box 491788, Los Angeles, CA 90049

www.empirebooks.net

First published in 2007 by Empire Books

First edition
06 05 04 03 02 01 00 99 98 97 1 3 5 7 9 10 8 6 4 2

Printed in the United States of America.
Empire Books
P.O. Box 491788
Los Angeles, CA 90049
www.empirebooks.net

ISBN-13: 978-1-933901-26-8
ISBN-10: 1-933901-26-8

Library of Congress Cataloging-in-Publication Data

Kwok, Samuel.
   Mastering wing chun kung fu / by Samuel Kwok & Tony Massengill. -- 1st ed.
      p. cm.
   ISBN 978-1-933901-26-8 (pbk. : alk. paper)
   1. Kung fu. I. Massengill, Tony. II. Title. III. Title: Wing chun kung fu.
   GV1114.7.K85 2007
   796.815'9--dc22

2007011680

Dedication

This book is dedicated to the late Grandmaster Ip Man who spent his life promoting the Wing Chun Kung Fu system.

Acknowledgements

Samuel Kwok

I'd like to express my sincerest thanks to all those who have made the creation of this book possible.

My wife Xin Lou Kwok, my son Jason, my daughter Annie, and my stepson Dong Ni. I need to thank my parents Rev. Henry Kwok and Mrs Annie Wai Chun Kwok, my brothers and sisters, especially my brother John, for their support.

I would like to take this opportunity to thank the two men responsible for my education in the Ip Man Wing Chun system. I have been very fortunate in having the opportunity to train under both sons of the late Grandmaster Ip Man. Grandmasters Ip Chun and Ip Ching, both great Kung Fu men, and genuine gentlemen.

It is thanks to their generous attitudes and personalities that I was given unique access to the knowledge passed to them through their father. In addition to the knowledge they have also shared their family's heritage. Ip Ching's gift to me of his father's Knives as well as copies of the manuals passed from Leung Jan to Leung Bik to Ip Man to Ip Ching and now to me, there are no words that can say thank you enough. I can only promise to do all within my power to help properly pass this rich heritage to the next generation.

I have also benefited from the knowledge and experience of other Ip Man students, such as Chan Wai Hong, Wong Shun Leung, Tsiu Sheng Tin, Lok Yiu, and Lee Sing. I also owe these men a debt of gratitude.

I would like to pay my respects to the late Carlson Gracie. He and I conducted seminars together and built a friendship based on mutual respect for each other as people and as martial artists.

Also a special thank you to the staff at Empire Media, Jose Fraguas, Val Mijailovic and Michael James. Your professionalism has been outstanding. Thank you for producing the best products in the industry.

I'd like to say a special thanks to my disciple Tony Massengill whose help has been most valuable. Thanks also to Dan Knight, Anthony Warwick, and Sara Lai and Juan Jose Bonet Vidal for their help with this book. I also thank Trevor Jefferson, Peter Jones, Stephen Dyde, Martin Brieley, Billy Davidson, Paul Smith, Guy Diddcot, Philip Nearing, Martin Lloyd, and all my instructors around the world who continue to spread and preserve the traditional Ip Man Wing Chun system. Then last, but by no means least may I thank all my loyal students whose determination to learn, honor, and preserve this traditional Chinese martial art is wonderful to see.

Tony Massengill

Anytime a project like this is undertaken, there are many people to thank. Those who have directly impacted the project, as well as those who have made a contribution in an indirect way. So I would like to make the following attempt to thank those who have directly impacted this project or have indirectly impacted this project by way of their impact on my life both in and out of the martial arts. First of all I would like to thank God, and my Lord, Jesus Christ, without whom I could accomplish nothing.

I would like to thank my beautiful Wife, Yongnan for her love, understanding and support in my pursuit and training in Wing Chun.

I need to thank my teacher, Grandmaster Samuel Kwok, who accepted me as his disciple and gave me his family name (Kwok Ching Yin.) He has been the embodiment of the term Sifu (Teacher/Father.) Grandmaster Kwok has been very giving, caring, and nurturing in his teaching and explaining the keys of the Wing Chun system.

I would like to say thank you to my Sigungs (Kung Fu Grandfathers) Grandmasters Ip Chun and Ip Ching, for their generous instruction in their father's Kung Fu method.

In the forty plus years I have been involved in training in the Martial Arts, there have been far too many to mention who have shared their knowledge and insight, and to them I say thank you. Of these I owe a special thank you to a man who has been my mentor, friend, councilor, and who has become my big brother, Glen Moore.

I would like to also say a special thank you to some of my students who have helped in many ways ranging from proof reading some of this work to running my classes while I was busy writing. So to Tim Phillips, Chris Gibbs, Lafayette Harris and Jeff Benton…Thank You!

I must also thank the staff at Empire Media, Jose Fraguas ,Val Mijailovic and Michael James. Working with Empire Media was a great experience.

Finally I wish to thank my pastor, Ron Johnson and his wife Sandy, of Bethel Temple Assembly of God, in Hampton Virginia, for their teaching and leadership.

CONTENTS

About the Authors

Grandmaster Samuel Kwok

Samuel Kwok is a 2nd Generation Master of Wing Chun Kung Fu under the tradition passed through the Ip Man Family. He was born in Hong Kong in 1948, the son of a Church Minister. He became interested in the martial arts at an early age. His formal introduction to the martial arts was in the White Crane Kung Fu system, under the guidance of his uncle Luk Chi Fu. His Wing Chun training began in 1967 under Chan Wai Ling in Hong Kong.

In 1972 Samuel Kwok moved from Hong Kong to the United Kingdom to study and pursue a career in psychiatric nursing. While living in London, he went to the Church of Reverend Kao, who was a good friend of this father. Reverend Kao told him about one of the members of the congregation, who was a Wing Chun teacher named Lee Sing. Lee Sing was a student of Sifu Lok Yiu and Chiu Wan. Before Lee Sing left Hong Kong he became a student of Ip Man. Furthermore, while in Hong Kong, Lee Sing also learned Leung Jan style Wing Chun. After meeting Lee Sing, Samuel Kwok became his student in 1973. Samuel Kwok began teaching in 1975. He started by teaching his friends and fellow student nurses from the hospital, but later went onto teaching the general public.

Samuel Kwok was confused by the fact that everyone's Wing Chun Forms were different, so in 1978 he returned to Hong Kong in the hope of finding the true source of Wing Chun. Samuel Kwok was introduced by Lee Sing to Grandmaster Ip Man's eldest son, Grandmaster Ip Chun. It was later, during their second meeting that Ip Chun offered to teach Samuel Kwok the wooden dummy techniques. Samuel Kwok realized that he was being given a great honor, so he accepted. At this time, Ip Chun was only teaching part time.

For the next few years Samuel Kwok had private tuition from Ip Chun, and after gaining Master level in Wing Chun, he opened his first school in Hong Kong. It was not long before his students began making a name for themselves at tournaments and demonstrations in the colony.

Before returning to the UK, Master Kwok made a vow to Ip Chun that he would promote his master and Wing Chun throughout the world. Upon returning to the UK in 1981, he was appointed as the chairman and senior overseas representative of the Ip Chun Martial Art Association by Grandmaster Ip Chun.

After settling in the UK, Master Kwok began to teach Wing Chun privately. Later, he opened his first school because of the great demand for his instruction. After settling in the UK, Master Kwok started teaching first in St.Annes-on-sea, then in Manchester, and later throughout the country. In 1985, in his effort to promote Traditional Wing Chun and his Si-Fu, Master Kwok held the first of many seminars in the UK for Grandmaster Ip Chun.

In 1986 Master Kwok's first book "The Path to Wing Chun" was published, which has sold many copies all over the world. It has helped beginners and martial artists from different styles to understand the art of Wing Chun kung fu. It has been so successful that it is currently in its 6th edition, often been reprinted to keep it up to date.

In 1983 The Chinese society of Lancaster University invited Samuel Kwok to teach Wing Chun to university students. This was a great success, and in later years students at the university set up a Lancaster University Wing Chun Club. Master Kwok still teaches at the university club to this day, and the average yearly membership of this club often sores well over 100 members.

In 1992 Master Kwok invited both Grandmasters Ip Chun and Ip Ching to the UK to hold their first joint seminars across the country. It was during this visit that Master Kwok was able to begin learning from Grandmaster Ip Ching as well. This was Grandmaster Ip Ching's first visit to the UK.

In 1994 Master Kwok returned to Hong Kong, and at the suggestion of Grandmaster Ip Chun, resumed training with his brother, Grandmaster Ip Ching, in order to gain a different perspective on the Wing Chun system. That same year Master Kwok helped to organize some very successful seminars in America, taught by Grandmaster Ip Chun.

In December of 1994 Master Kwok became an honorary chief instructor of Yunan Zhong Hua Wushu Academy. The position was given to Master Kwok in recognition of his success in spreading Chinese martial arts to the West.

In 1995, once again Grandmaster Ip Ching was invited by Master Kwok to the UK to conduct several seminars across the country, but this time he was accompanied by Grandmaster Chu Sheung Tin, one of the first students in Hong Kong of the late Grandmaster Ip Man.

Also in 1995, the two famous brothers Grandmaster Ip Chun and Ip Ching were brought to Chicago by Samuel Kwok to teach together for the first time in America.

In 1998 Master Samuel Kwok received a BA honors from Manchester University for his life time achievement and promotion of martial arts. Today Master Kwok is constantly promoting Wing Chun across the world by conducting and organizing seminars, competitions, demonstrations, as well as producing books and videos with Empire Media.

In 1999 Samuel Kwok performed demonstrations with his students at the 1st World Ving Tsun Conference, which was held in Hong Kong. The success of this led to Samuel Kwok also performing again at the 2nd World Ving Tsun Conference. Samuel Kwok sees the conferences as a great opportunity to promote Ip Man's Wing Chun in a way that Ip Man would be proud of.

In 2001 Samuel Kwok and many of his students and instructors from around the world once again showed their dedication to Ip Family Wing Chun by traveling to Fat Shan in Southern China to help Grandmaster Ip Ching promote the Ip Man Tong. They performed demonstrations to help promote the opening of the museum dedicated to Ip Man, which was opened in 2002.

Master Kwok also runs a yearly training camp in Mallorca, where students and instructors from around the world can come to perfect their skills in the art of Wing Chun.

Master Kwok also helps to arrange tours and training in Hong Kong with Grandmasters Ip Chun and Ip Ching for his students, showing that like himself, he wants his students to benefit from this great master first hand.

Master Kwok is the leader of the **Traditional Ip Man Wing Chun Association** with schools around the world. Those interested in more information on Master Samuel Kwok, or information on authorized instructors around the world can visit:

www.ipmanwingchun.com

Grandmaster Samuel Kwok is available for private tuition,
seminars and instructor tuition.
For details feel free to contact Grandmaster Kwok directly:
Phone – 07856265889 or – 07753191680
Or email: kwokwingchun@hotmail.com
www.kwokwingchun.com

Sifu Tony Massengill

Tony has been involved in the martial arts for over forty years, and has earned Black Belt rank or instructor certification in several disciplines, including Chin-Na, Kenpo, Thai Boxing, Tae Kwon Do, and various stick and knife systems.

He is retired from a career in public safety where he worked for over twenty-five years serving as a police officer, fire fighter, and emergency medic. Over the span of his career he developed training programs and taught many in the field of law enforcement, emergency medical services, and the military.

Tony began training in the Wing Chun Kung Fu system in 1979. Over the years that have passed he has trained with several instructors, but finally found a home under Master Samuel Kwok. Tony was accepted as a private disciple and was eventually awarded Master level certification by Master Kwok in June 2005.

When asked about his background and his experience under Master Kwok, Tony states, "I have been involved in the martial arts since the age of five. After training extensively in many fighting methods, I settled on Wing Chun as the system I felt was the best for my goals, which was combat effectiveness in the street, not the ring. But settling on Wing Chun was just the beginning of my journey.

After pursuing Wing Chun under many instructors, several of which were very well known, I had the opportunity to meet and experience Master Kwok's Wing Chun, and immediately knew I had found what I was looking for. I had worked for many years as a public safety professional, so I knew what REAL fights were on the streets, so I am not easily impressed by instructors demonstrating their supposed "Deadly Effectiveness." But with Samuel Kwok's Wing Chun, I was blown away. This feeling was further solidified when I was in Hong Kong and Foshan, China with Master Kwok. I saw first hand how much respect everyone there has for this great Kung Fu man.

Tony was selected to be Grandmaster Kwok's demonstration partner at the 2nd World Wing Chun Conference held in Hong Kong in 2005. Tony is the senior U.S. Representative of Grandmaster Kwok and has been appointed to administer Kwok's association in the United States.

Tony resides in Gloucester, Virginia U.S.A. and teaches Wing Chun full-time at his school **MASS Martial Arts**, in Yorktown, Virginia, the U.S. Headquarters of the **Traditional Ip Man Wing Chun Association**, founded by Grandmaster Kwok.

Those interested in contacting Tony Massengill can visit his school's web site at: **www.massmartialarts.com** or e-mail him at: **sifu@massmartialarts.com**
Or call (757) 846-1188

Statement by Grandmaster Samuel Kwok

I would like to take this opportunity to thank the two men responsible for my education in the Ip Man Wing Chun system. I have been very fortunate in having the opportunity to train under both sons of the late Grandmaster Ip Man. Grandmasters Ip Chun and Ip Ching, both great Gung Fu men, and genuine gentlemen. It is thanks to their generous attitudes and personalities that I was given unique access to the knowledge passed to them through their father. Grandmaster Ip Man was fortunate in having access to the knowledge and skills developed by two Masters, Chan Wah Shun and Leung Bik. He was able to glean great insight into the differences in application due to the much different physical stature of these two Masters. I too have been fortunate in being introduced to the nuances in application of the Ip brothers, as they each have a unique prospective and approach to the application of their fathers method due to their physical stature and attributes. I have been given the benefit of their knowledge, skill and experience. For this I will forever be grateful to both Ip Chun and Ip Ching.

—Samuel Kwok

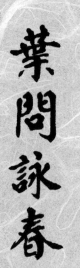

Note on Spelling

In the translation of many of the Chinese terms into English, the reader may find some inconsistencies in spelling. For example, the term Sao translates as "hand" as in Chi Sao, "sticking hands." However it is popular to render the spelling of this term as either "Sao" or "Sau." I have found that I often use the two interchangeably in my personal notes and writings.

This inconsistency of spelling Chinese terms in English is very prevalent in writings on the subject of Wing Chun. Even the name Wing Chun has many different spellings in English. There is the popular Wing Chun which we use here, there is also Ving Tsun, Yong Chun, Ving Chun, and the list goes on and on.

The problem is in attempting to spell a Chinese term in the way it sounds to the English speaker. For instance, if you didn't know the proper spelling of car, you could easily spell it "kar" based on the way it sounds.

Throughout this book we have attempted to maintain a consistent spelling of Chinese terms, however there may be some instances where I have failed in this attempt. For this I take full responsibility and apologize in advance.

However as an excuse I must point out that we are talking about the English language, where the word "phonetically" means to spell a word the way it sounds. But if you spelled "phonetically" the way it sounds, you would most likely spell it "Fonetically" which would be wrong, which spelled phonetically would be "rong."

—Tony Massengill

Wing Chun Code of Conduct

The Wing Chun Code of Conduct Said to have originated with Leung Jan and passed to the current generation by Ip Man, serves as a reminder to all practitioners that their martial art represents more than just fighting. It requires the acceptance of a strong moral philosophy framed in courage, honor, ethics and humble etiquette. Wing Chun must be preserved for warriors, not bullies and braggarts. Living this Code of Honor is the way of the warrior.

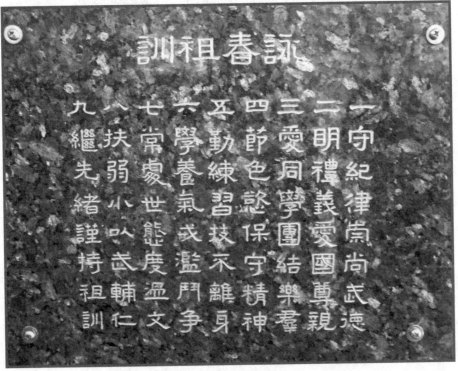

This is the marble display of the Code of Conduct that hangs at the Hong Kong Athletic Association.

守 紀 律 崇 尚 武 德
sáu　géi　leuht　sùhng　seuhng　móuh　däk

Remain disciplined – uphold yourself ethically as a martial artist

明 禮 義 愛 國 尊 親
mìhng　láih　yih　ngoi　gwok　jyùn　chàn

Practice courtesy and righteousness – serve the community and honor your family

愛 同 學 團 結 樂 群
ngoi　tùhng　hohk　tyùhn　git　lohk　kwahn

Love your fellow students or classmates – be united and avoid conflicts

節 色 慾 保 守 精 神
jit　sĭk　yuhk　bóu　sáu　jìng　sàhn

Limit your desires and pursuit of bodily pleasures – preserve the proper spirit

勤 練 習 技 不 離 身
kàhn　lihn　jaahp　geih　bät　léih　sàn

Train diligently and make it a habit – maintain your skills

學 養 氣 救 濫 鬥 民
hohk　yéuhng　hei　gau　laahm　dau　màhn

Learn to develop spiritual tranquility – abstain from arguments and fights

常 處 世 態 度 溫 民
sèyhng　chyu　sai　taai　douh　wàn　màhn

Participate in society – be conservative, cultured and gentle in your manners

扶 弱 小 以 武 輔 仁
fùh　yeuhk　síu　yíh　móuh　fuh　yàhn

Help the weak and the very young – use your martial skill for the good of humanity

繼 光 緒 漢 持 祖 訓
gai　gwòng　séuih　hon　chìh　jóu　fan

Pass on the tradition – preserve this Chinese art and its Rules of Conduct

Foreword by Grandmaster Ip Chun

Ip Chun with Samuel Kwok at the Athletic Association in Hong Kong.

I conducted my first Wing Chun seminar in June of 1985 in the city of Leeds, United Kingdom. The last seminar was held in September of 2001 in Portsmouth, UK. During this time, I visited England and the United Kingdom at least once a year and held over 200 seminars within 20 major cities. More than 100,000 Wing Chun practitioners have attended the seminars, and Samuel Kwok has dedicated his time and effort in helping me to organize these seminars.

Throughout those 17 years, on many occasions I lectured on Wing Chun's principles and theories, which I have acquired through many years of Wing Chun study and vast personal experience. Alongside, I also had Samuel Kwok, my loyal student. Samuel became mytranslator, both on a social level and as my interpreter for the correct principles and theories of Wing Chun as passed down by my father, Ip Man.

Samuel first had to understand my teachings in order to accurately translate my instruction for the English audience. Consequently, Samuel Kwok was the first to benefit from my seminars, and was able to gain additional Wing Chun insight and knowledge.

In the 1980s, Samuel Kwok published a very popular book, *The Path to Wing Chun*. This book has sold all over the world and has become well known for its clear, instructive insight into the art of Wing Chun.

Over the last twenty years Samuel Kwok has further studied my teaching, and has multiplied and refined his Wing Chun knowledge and skills. His second book will therefore offer a deeper understanding and refinement of Wing Chun as taught by my father and the Ip family. This will prove to be a publication of great benefit and recommended reading for all who study and practice Wing Chun.

—*Ip Chun*

Foreword By Grandmaster Ip Ching

It is with the greatest of pleasure that I write this foreword for Samuel Kwok.

Samuel has been studying and teaching Ip Man Wing Chun since the early 1980's and has helped spread the Ip family system in the United Kingdom, Europe, America and a host of other countries. In 1991 Samuel invited me to host the first of my many seminars in the United Kingdom, followed by my first seminar in America back in 1995. It was Samuel who organized, translated and assisted me in the demonstrations and applications of my teachings at these seminars.

Ip Ching with Samuel Kwok at his home in Hong Kong.

Samuel has continued to visit me over the years in Hong Kong and he and his students have taken part in the 1st and 2nd World Ving Tsun Conference and represented the Ip Man system at numerous demonstrations in Hong Kong and the Ip Man Tong Museum in Foshan, China.

He continues to pass on the Ip Man teachings to his students and travels regularly to many countries to support his instructors in providing a high standard of instruction. His enthusiasm never ceases!

I have a high regard for his knowledge and understanding of the Ip Man system and I wholly endorse him and his book which will aid the understanding of the Ip Man Wing Chun Kung Fu system to whomever reads this book.

—Ip Ching

Introduction

A Key is by definition a tool used to gain entry into an area that is locked and otherwise inaccessible. In this book we will introduce the reader to the keys of the Ip Man Wing Chun Kung Fu system. These keys unlock the hidden meaning, understanding and power of this great martial art.

Wing Chun as we know it today has been passed from the warriors of the past, to the present generation of masters, as a very comprehensive, economical, and practical system of combat. While other methods of martial art have been adapted, changed and watered-down to become modern sports, or just forms of physical exercise with little relationship to combat, Wing Chun is a combat system in every sense of the word.

Wing Chun falls into a category known as Southern Shaolin Boxing (known for having fast hands and strong leg techniques). Kung fu methods are usually listed as being either hard or soft in application. Wing Chun is actually a good balance of both.

We use the word "system" on purpose. A system is something that can be defined. It has a specific set of components which are consistent. According to various dictionaries, a system is "an organized set of doctrines, ideas, or principles usually intended to explain the arrangement or working of a systematic whole." So as you can see, in order to be a system, there must be well defined boundaries and components which comprise the "unified whole." There must be a standard by which the "system" is performed.

One of the reasons for writing this book is to set in print the standard of the Wing Chun system as passed to me through the sons of Grandmaster Ip Man. This is important as there is a lot of confusion as to just what is, and what is not Wing Chun.

Let me begin by saying that there are many very good and ethical Wing Chun instructors in the world. But unfortunately there are many who do not fit into that category. In particular those who are teaching a spurious form of kung fu and using Ip Man's name to sell and / or justify what they are teaching.

I have often had the misfortune to see such schools in practice. The instructors of such schools claim to teach Wing Chun as it has been handed down by Ip Man. They often openly claim lineage through both of my sifus, Ip Chun and Ip Ching. However the standard of their teaching is often very poor. They claim the Grandmasters as their teachers but their only real connection is a photo opportunity in a seminar where they met them. These instructors now use the photos of them with the Grandmaster as a marketing tool to mislead students. I raised concern to my masters about this situation but the sad conclusion is that there is little that can be done to put a stop to this kind of misleading unscrupulous instructor. We do not live in old China, where you could go in and close these kind of schools down. In today's world this cannot be done, therefore the only option open to us here is of course to educate!

The only defense against these kinds of dishonest instructors is to educate the public as to the authentic standard of the Wing Chun system as passed down by Grandmaster Ip Man. This is the reason for the work you now hold in your hands. It is the sincere hope of the authors that we can in some small way help those who really want to learn the heritage and tradition that is the Ip Man Wing Chun Kung Fu system.

CHAPTER 1

Wing Chun's History

Chinese martial arts are full of exciting stories of the origins of the various systems. Wing Chun is no different. Finding the true history of Wing Chun, or many other Chinese kung fu systems is difficult due to the lack of written records. Stories of the origin have been passed down orally from master to disciple for centuries. Thus, it is possible that names, places, and events are inaccurate.

The stories handed down through the generations hold that the Wing Chun system was developed in the famous Siu Lum (Shaolin) Temple. The system was said to have been taught to a young woman named Yim Wing Chun by a Siu Lum nun named Ng Mui. Yim Wing Chun eventually married a martial artist named Leung Bok Cho, to whom she taught the method. Leung Bok Cho in turn taught Leung Lan Kwai, Leung Yee Tai, Wong Wah Bo, and others. Leung Yee Tai and Wong Wah Bo taught Leung Jan, who became a famous fighter and Chinese doctor. Leung Jan taught his son Leung Bik, as well as a merchant named Chan Wah Shun. Ip Man was passed the system first by Chan Wah Shun, and then later in Hong Kong by Leung Bik.

There are many books and articles which debate the history listed above. As we have pointed out, with the lack of written records, there is no way of knowing just how accurate this account is. There is also nothing to be gained by arguing over it. So instead of debating the uncertain history of this great system, we will concentrate on what we know to be fact. The Wing Chun system as it has been passed down from the late Grandmaster Ip Man up to the present generation, through the teaching of his sons, Grandmasters Ip Chun and Ip Ching.

Ip Man was the first to openly teach Wing Chun. He began his teaching career in Foshan, China, and then later in Hong Kong. It is through Ip Man's teaching that Wing Chun has spread throughout the world. Ip Man had many students, but it was Bruce Lee, the famous movie star and "King of Kung Fu" who was the most notable. It was through the fame brought by Bruce Lee that the world became aware of Wing Chun and Lee's teacher, Grandmaster Ip Man.

According to the accounts given to Ip Man's sons Ip Chun and Ip Ching (by Ip Man), their father began his training as a young boy.

Ip Man (1893–1972) was born at Song Yuen of Foshan, China at the end of the Qing Dynasty. Foshan was situated at the most prosperous region of the Guangdong province. Well known masters of the Southern kung fu schools, Wong Fai-hung, Cheung Hung-shing, Leung Jan, Leung Siu-ching etc. came from Foshan. Ip Man grew up hearing the stories of the exploits of these great kung fu men. So it's not surprising that he would develop into one of the legendary masters himself.

Ip Man's education in Wing Chun began as a youth when he became a student of Chan Wah Shun, who was a student of the famous Leung Jan. Chan Wah Shun rented the Ip family clan hall on the main street of Foshan in order to teach kung fu. He accepted Ip Man as a student towards the end of his teaching career when he was quite old. Master Chan was a big man by Chinese standards, so his kung fu was powerful. Ip Man learned from Master Chan until the masters' death, and continued his training with his Sihing (Senior) Ng Chun until Ip Man left Foshan for Hong Kong in 1941.

Ip Man moved to Hong Kong at the age of 15 to attend St. Stephens College. There he had a chance meeting with an old gentleman who was a martial artist. This old man crossed hands with Ip Man and beat him soundly. This disturbed Ip Man very much as he had developed his kung fu to a high level and considered himself to be quite proficient. As it turned out, the old gentleman was Leung Bik, the son of Ip Man's Sifu, Master Chan Wah Shun's teacher, the famous Leung Jan.

Master Leung Bik's Wing Chun was much more refined than what Ip Man had learned from Master Chan. While Chan Wah Shun had been a big man,

Leung Bik was much smaller. There was also a pretty wide gap in the education level between the two masters. Chan Wah Shun was not very well educated, while Leung Bik was the son of Leung Jan, who was a well educated doctor of Chinese medicine. This education was passed to his son. This meant that Leung Bik was better able to understand the underlying principals of the Wing Chun system. This knowledge was passed to Ip Man.

Upon learning all that Leung Bik had to teach him, Ip Man went on to explore ways to simplify Wing Chun, making it easier to understand. In addition to his education in "Wing Chun," Ip Man received an advanced formal education in his youth. He learned the theories and principals of modern science and could therefore make use of modern technological knowledge such as mechanical and mathematical theories to explain the principals of Wing Chun. Ip Man even changed terminology such as "The Five Elements," and "Eight Diagrams" (Ba Gua) which were commonly used in metaphysics. This helped to demystify Wing Chun, thus making it easier for the common student to understand and apply the system.

After completing his Wing Chun education under Leung Bik, Ip Man returned to China. Back in Foshan, Ip Man began teaching a small group of students, including Kwok Fu and Luen Kai. In 1949 Ip Man returned to live in Hong Kong, where he eventually began his public instruction of Wing Chun.

In July 1950, through Lee Man's introduction, Grandmaster Ip Man started teaching in Dai Lam Street, Kowloon. The first Wing Chun Kung Fu class was for the Restaurant Workers Association. When he opened the class there was only 8 people, including Leung Shang and Lok Yiu. All these were restaurant workers, but later he was joined by Chu Shung Tin, Yip Bo Ching, Chiu Wan, Lee Yan Wing, Law Peng, Man Siu Hung, and others. Grandmaster Ip Man also taught in the Restaurant Workers Shang Wan branch, Union HQ in Hong Kong. Students included Lee Wing, Yue May Keng, Lee Leung Foon, and others.

Over the next 20 years Ip Man would leave his mark on the world of martial arts by teaching those that would spread Wing Chun across the globe. Some of those who became students of the Grandmaster were Wong Shun Leung, Bruce Lee, and of course Ip Man's sons, Ip Chun and Ip Ching.

The Ip Man Wing Chun system has today become one of the most popular martial art systems in the world. Bruce Lee was initially responsible for bringing Wing Chun to the attention of the world, but it has been through the teaching of today's masters, and most notably Ip Man's sons Ip Chun and Ip Ching that we have full knowledge of the heritage of this great kung fu system.

Ip Man with his most personal students, his sons (L) Ip Ching and (R) Ip Chun.

Wing Chun History by Ip Man

The founder of the Ving Tsun Kung fu System, Miss Yim Ving Tsun was a native of Canton China. As a young girl, she was intelligent and athletic, upstanding and manly. She was betrothed to Leung Bok Chau, a salt merchant of Fukien. Soon after that, her mother died. Her father, Yim Yee, was wrongfully accused of a crime, and nearly went to jail. So the family moved far away, and finally settled down at the foot of Tai Leung Mountain at the Yunnan-Szechuan border. There, they earned a living by. All this happened during the reign of Emperor K'anghsi (1662–1722).

At the time, kung fu was becoming very strong in Siu Lam Monastery (Shaolin Monastery) of Mt. Sung, Honan. This aroused the fear of the Manchu government, which sent troops to attack the Monastery. They were unsuccessful. A man called Chan Man Wai was the First Placed Graduate of the Civil Service Examination that year. He was seeking favour with the government, and suggested a plan. He plotted with Siu Lam monk Ma Ning Yee and others. They set fire to the Monastery while soldiers attacked it from the outside. Siu Lam was burnt down, and the monks scattered. Buddhist Abbess Ng Mui, Abbot Chi Shin, Abbot Pak Mei, Master Fung To Tak and Master Miu Hin escaped and fled their separate ways.

Ng Mui took refuge in White Crane Temple on Mt. Tai Leung (also known as Mt. Chai Har). There she came to know Yim Yee and his daughter Yim Ving Tsun. She bought bean curds at their store. They became friends.

Ving Tsun was a young woman then, and her beauty attracted the attention of a local bully. He tried to force Ving Tsun to marry him. She and her father were very worried. Ng Mui learned of this and took pity on Ving Tsun. She agreed to teach Ving Tsun fighting techniques so that she could protect herself. Then she would be able to solve the problem with the bully, and marry Leung

The Hong Kong Athletic Association.

Bok Chau, her betrothed husband. So Ving Tsun followed Ng Mui into the mountains, and started to learn kung fu. She trained night and day, and mastered the techniques. Then she challenged the local bully to a fight and beat him. Ng Mui set off to travel around the country, but before she left, she told Ving Tsun to strictly honour the kung fu traditions, to develop her kung fu after her marriage, and to help the people working to overthrow the Manchu government and restore the Ming Dynasty. This is how Ving Tsun kung fu was handed down by Abbess Ng Mui.

After the marriage, Ving Tsun taught her Kung fu to her husband Leung Bok Chau, and he passed his kung fu techniques on to Leung Lan Kwai. Leung Lan Kwai passed it on to Wong Wah Bo. Wong Wah Bo was a member of an opera troupe on board a junk, known to the Chinese as the Red Junk. Wong worked on the Red Junk with Leung Yee Tei. It so happened that Abbot Chi Shin, who fled from Siu Lam, had disguised himself as a cook and was now working on the Red Junk. Chi Shin taught the Six-and-a-half Point Long Pole

The Ip Family.

Techniques to Leung Yee Tei. Wong Wah Bo was close to Leung Yee Tei, and they shared what they knew about kung fu. Together they correlated and improved their techniques, and thus the Six-and-half-point Long Pole Techniques were incorporated into Ving Tsun Kung fu.

Leung Yee Tei passed the Kung fu on to Leung Jan, a well known herbal doctor in Fat Shan. Leung Jan grasped the innermost secrets of Ving Tsun, and attained the highest level of proficiency. Many kung fu masters came to challenge him, but all were defeated. Leung Jan became very famous. Later, he passed his kung fu on to Chan Wah Shan, who took me as his student many decades ago. I studied kung fu alongside my kung fu brothers such as Ng Siu Lo, Ng Chung So, Chan Yu Min and Lui Yu Jai. Ving Tsun was thus passed down to us, and we are eternally grateful to our kung fu ancestors and teachers. We will always remember and appreciate our roots, and this shared feeling will always keep our kung fu brothers close together. This is why I am organizing the Ving Tsun Fellowship, and I hope my kung fu brothers will support me in this. This will be very important in the promotion of Kung fu.

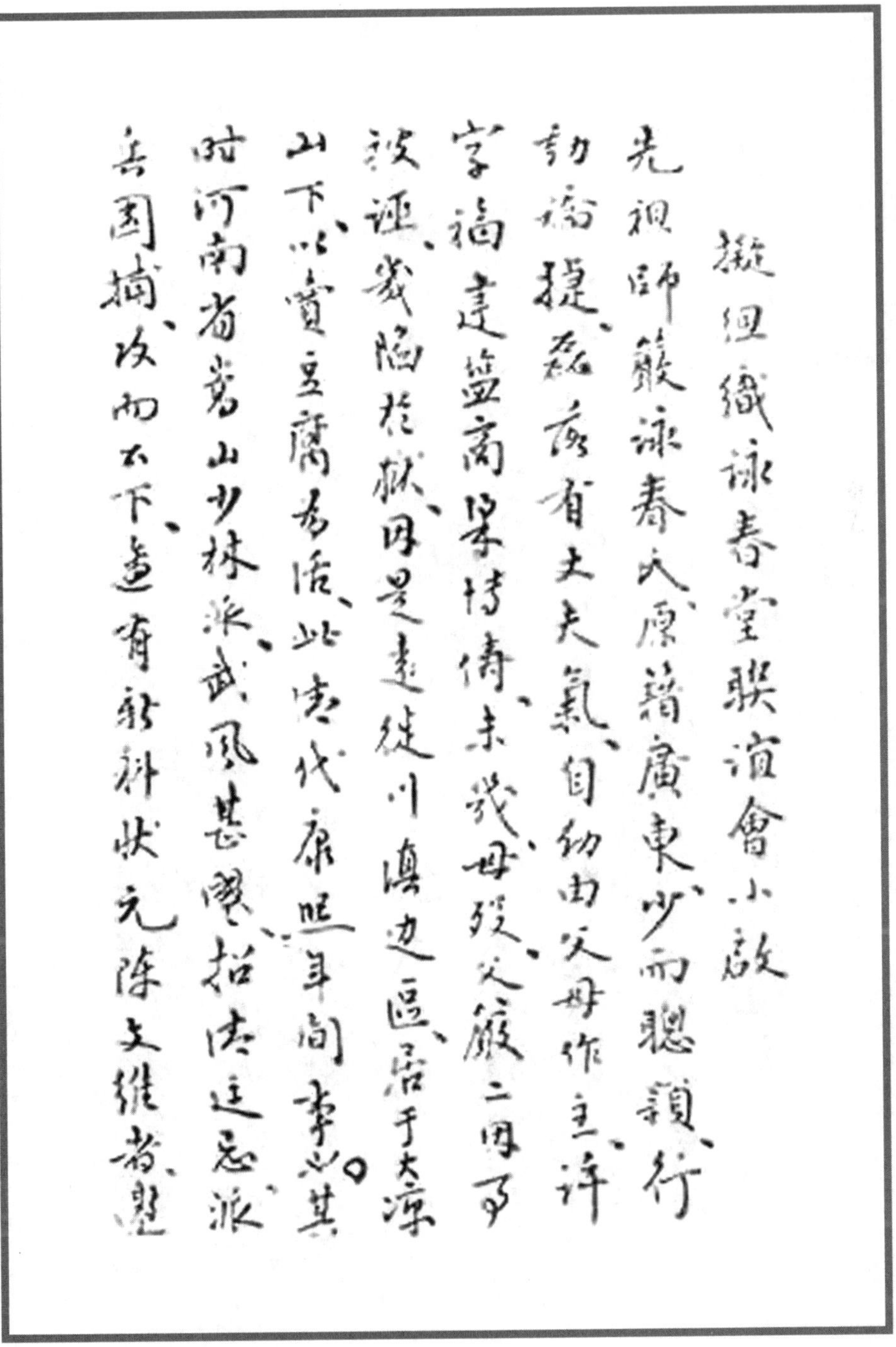

擬組織詠春堂聯誼會小啟

先祖師嚴詠春氏原籍廣東少而聰穎、
勤瑜提孺、廣有士夫氣自幼由父母作主許
字禍達鹽商梁博儔、未幾我母殘父嚴二事了
彼誣陷於獄、母是遠徒川漠邊區居于大涼
山下以賣豆腐為活、此清代康照年間事也其
時河南省嵩山少林派武風甚熾招倖延惹派
兵圍捕攻而不下遠有新科狀元陳文維者題

Ip Man's Handwritten History of Wing Chun.

葉問詠春

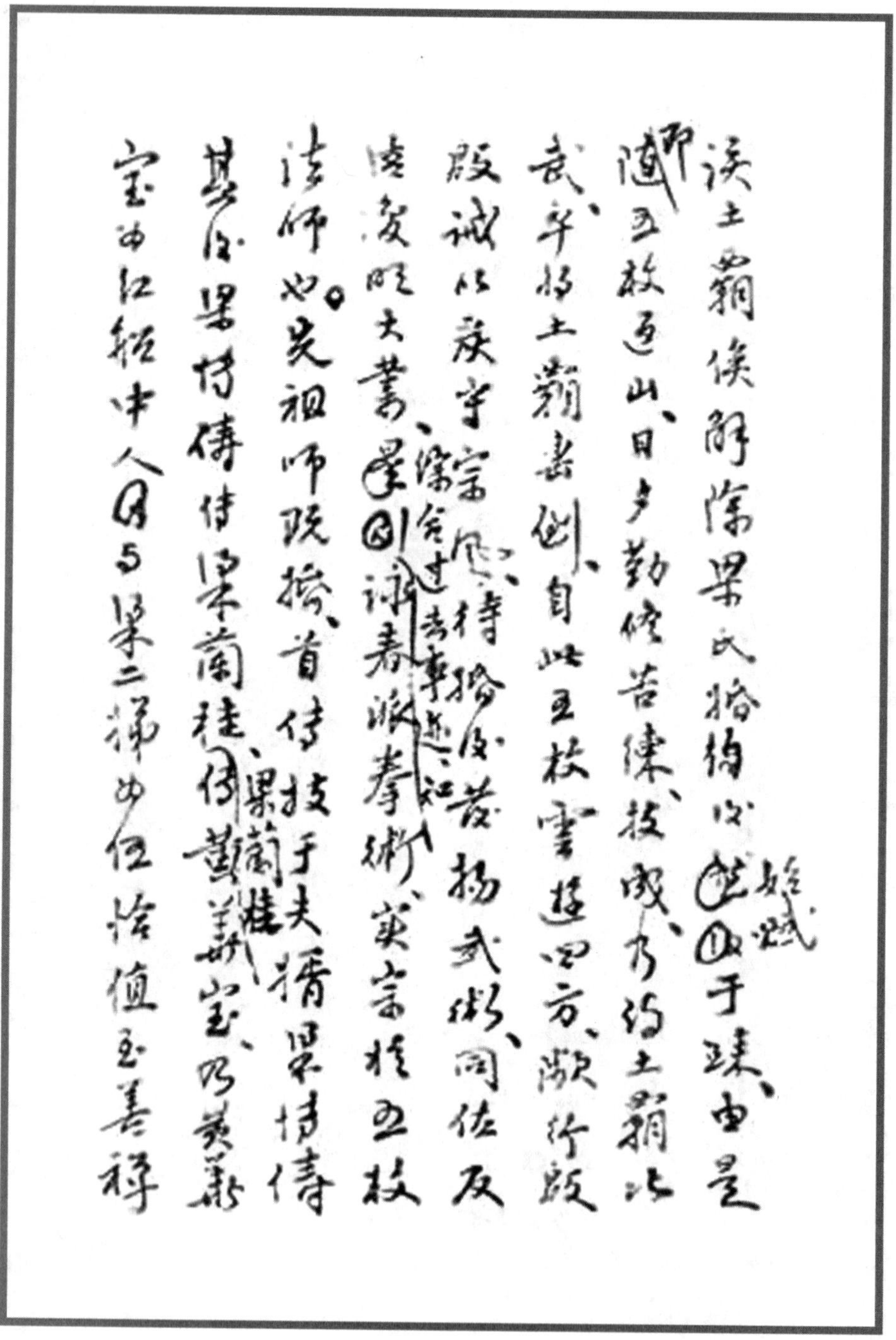

誤主霸侯群儒皆氏掉捣心　始戰　于殊申是

師遍五教逗山日夕勤修苦練技或为约土霸此

武平将土霸嘉倒自此五教雲遊四方歌行殿

殷诚以庚子家忌待搜皮若揚武術同佐及

廣發明大業學习詠春派拳術實宮於五教

法師也先祖師殷掛首侍技于夫橋果情傳

其尽果持傳侍梁蘭桂梁蘭桂侍蕭美宝乃黄華

宝女红船中人口5梁二弟此位拾值至善祥

竊獻議、誤傳句直寺僧、馬寧兒等、私廬縱大

裹庄外合少林寺被燬、修徒星散、由是五枚法

師与至善禅師、白眉禅師、馮道德、苗顯等五

人点点各筆走而五枚止于大涼山（又名槎查山）

白鶴觀、毎自下山以市、因与嚴二之女資易弼

五枚熟一时失祖師年已及祥省吉地上朔其近

其姿色博勢迫搶父女二人曰有夏色的五枚

汇師康素緣由、日悍其道、許以待技傍身、結

葉問詠春

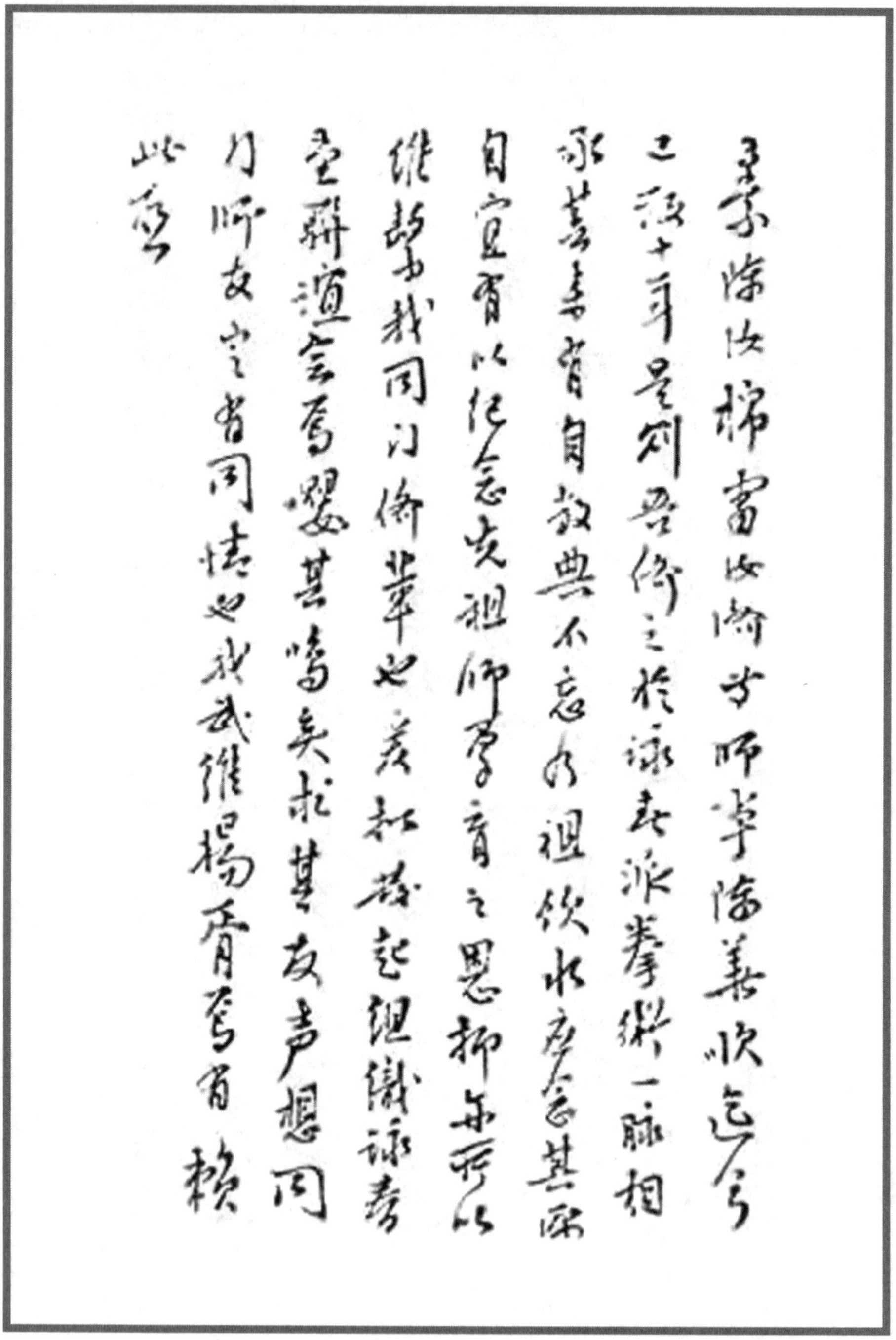

承除夜稟書以倚弍師辈臨善欣逢乎

之誼十年景列晉修之於詠春派拳術一脈相

承莫善育自敦典不忘水祖俶水彦念其所

自宜育以任念友祖師彦育之恩揚永垂於

維势我同門儕辈也羌和搽起粗織詠春

爰辦道会為嬰其嗚美求其友声想同

以師友之肯同情也我武維揚� 肯賴

此乎

師混跡紅船中為「煲頭」勝絕技以立半概付

與梁二娣而黃亦寶與二娣以其季紅船因

日久觀摩互相傳習補短截長渾成一体

從而詠春拳中④有六点半棍者盖首由此

迨至梁二娣传技于佛山名医梁墳先生果

贊溪乃對其奧道於化境遠近武士⑤慕名

春諸曰鬏雞為所改由是声名藉甚技素果

赞往於陳華順而间與師兄吳仲素吳小魯吳仲

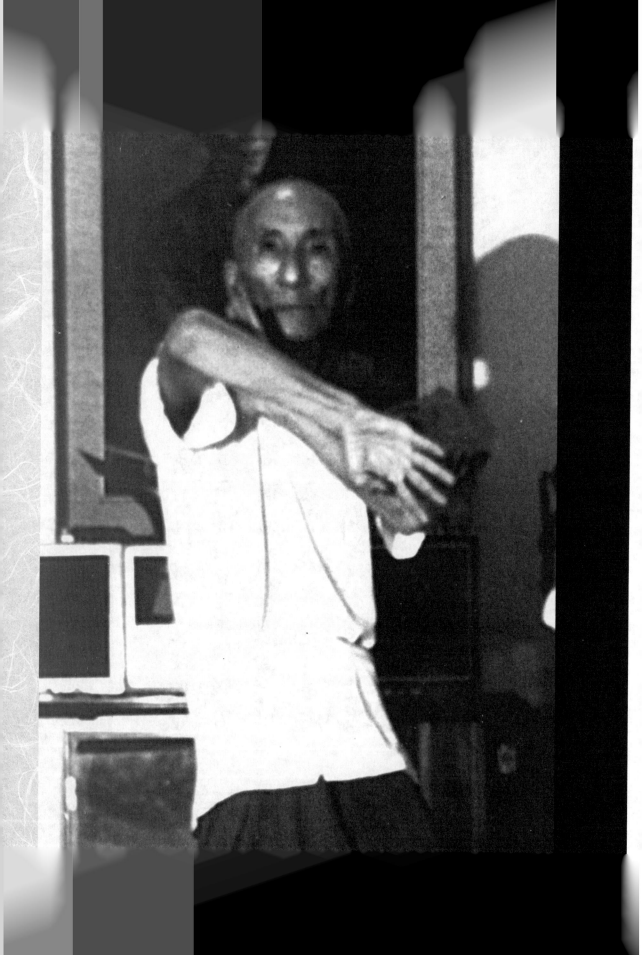

CHAPTER 2

Ip Man's Wing Chun ... What is it?

"Ip Man Wing Chun Kung Fu"... What is it? Is there a way to really know if one is learning the authentic method as taught by Ip Man? Why are there so many differences in the Wing Chun systems taught by people who were supposed to have learned from Ip Man?

There are lots of questions about this rather simple kung fu system. Well, let's look at some possible answers to these and other questions.

First of all, let's take the question of "What is Ip Man Wing Chun Kung Fu?" Like any other method of martial art, it is a system of combat. By system, what are we talking about? Well, a system is something that can be defined. The Wing Chun system is comprised of three hand forms, Siu Lim Tao, Chum Kiu, and Biu Gee. There is also a set of movements on the wooden dummy, as well as two weapon sets, Luk Deem Boon Kwun (Pole), and Bart Jam Dao (Knives).

Like any system, there is a standard way of performing the components. Now naturally there are going to be some slight differences in the way each person performs the movements. Subtle nuances in techniques based on the structure, stature, strengths and weaknesses of each individual practitioner. However, to be a "system" the components (Forms) should be pretty much the same from one instructor to the next. Slight differences may be anticipated,

葉問詠春拳

Grandmaster Ip Man training with his knives. These knives now belong to Master Samuel Kwok, part of the heritage passed to him by Grandmaster Ip Ching.

but generally one should be able to recognize the forms as being the same system if in fact they are the "Same System"!

The real problem with the Ip Man Wing Chun system is the sudden fame and interest brought to the system by the sudden death of kung fu superstar Bruce Lee, who was a student of Ip Man. Prior to Bruce Lee's death, Ip Man's Wing Chun was essentially a Hong Kong based system. There was no question as to who was in charge, and people setting themselves up as instructors prior to completing their training was not much of a problem. But with the death of Bruce Lee, just seven months after the death of Grandmaster Ip Man, there was a sudden interest in Wing Chun all over the world, and no way of checking on the level of knowledge of those who were claiming to teach the system.

The year was 1973. The internet did not exist, so unlike today, there was no way of instantly checking someone's claim of lineage and level of instruction. There was also the language barrier. It was hard for someone in the United States for example, to call Hong Kong and trace the history of someone claiming to teach under the authority of Ip Man. So over the years many instructors, who had not actually completed their education in Ip Man's Wing Chun system, established themselves as instructors. What they had not learned of the system, they simply made up on their own, and because there was no way of checking, students were easily misled.

Over the years, as more information became available about the Wing Chun system, students began to see that their instructor was teaching a much different version of Wing Chun than other instructors who had supposedly learned under the same instructor, Ip Man. So when questions were raised, the instructors would often cover for their fraudulent teachings by claiming that Ip Man taught them the "Secret Real" Wing Chun, and that everyone else had been taught a phony method by the Grandmaster. Thus began the confusion of the Wing Chun system.

Fortunately, Ip Man left a record of his system. Ten days before his death he recorded on 8mm film his Siu Lim Tao, Chum Kiu, and wooden dummy forms. His sons Ip Chun and Ip Ching continue to teach the system as their father taught them. So we know what the standard of the system is. The film of Ip Man causes a problem for many of the instructors mentioned above, who were misleading their students. Many were caught by surprise by the existence of the film, and the claims of their level of training and the methods they teach could now be compared to the standard left by Ip Man himself.

This problem was addressed by Ip Man's eldest son, Grandmaster Ip Chun in *Qi Magazine* in an article titled "The Spread of Wing Chun." In this article the Grandmaster stated, "students who had not completed the system would add things themselves to try and complete their system." The first two forms, especially the first form Siu Lim Tao, had been completed by most, and so these would all be the same. However, since they did not know the later forms, such as Biu Jee and the knives, they had to create their own forms rather than admit that they did not know them. The difference in teachers is due to their own making; this is why we have so many "styles" of Wing Chun.

The Grandmaster went on to explain, "The worst thing that happens is when someone asks why you're Wing Chun is different from another teacher's Wing Chun." However, the teacher will never say that he made this part up himself and would say that Ip Man personally taught them these different forms in secret. In saying this, the teacher does not realize that he is in fact ruining the reputation of his own Sifu, Ip Man, and his attitude to teaching. When Ip Man was teaching he would never teach one person a special technique that he would not show to others. He thought to do this was immoral, he treated everyone the same. He said, "I hope that in the future people will not continue on this path and keep saying these things, as it damages my father's image and is morally wrong."

Hopefully this explanation has answered some of the earlier questions about the system of Ip Man Wing Chun. In this book we will present the Ip Man Wing Chun system as it has been passed down in a direct line from Grandmaster Ip Man, through his most personal students, his sons Grandmasters Ip Chun and Ip Ching, and through their disciple, Grandmaster Samuel Kwok.

CHAPTER 3

The Learning Process

In the self-improvement classic "The New Psycho-Cybernetics—The Original Science of Self-Improvement" by Maxwell Maltz, there is an explanation of what Maltz calls the four stages of learning.

These four levels explain the progression from knowing nothing of the skill, to mastery of the skill. If studied, these four levels can be seen to be present in any physical skill development. In kung fu, these levels are very important as they can outline exactly when a skill can be relied upon in a violent encounter.

In the martial arts we begin by teaching the most basic of methods using a stair step process to advance to more advanced skills. Mastery is judged not by knowing, or being able to perform a technique, but in how the technique can be relied upon under surprise attack in a very dynamic and violent setting. The mere knowledge of and ability to perform a technique when given time to think about the method, is utterly useless in a fighting situation. The technique must "perform itself" in order to be relied upon.

Dr. Maltz explains the four stages of learning as follows:

• Unconscious Incompetence
• Conscious Incompetence
• Conscious Competence
• Unconscious Competence

Ip Man training on the Wooden Dummy. Taken during the filming of the 8MM made for his sons just 10 days prior to his death in 1972.

As you review these four levels, you can see the progression. As a student of the martial arts, we come into the school generally thinking we know at least how to do some rudimentary skills like punching. But upon being taught the proper method of punching, which includes such considerations as balance, power generation, and angle of execution, we realize that we didn't really know how to throw a punch.

At this time we pass from level one (Unconscious Incompetence) to level two (Conscious Incompetence). We now know that we do not know how to throw a proper punch. So we go about learning the proper mechanics of the technique. As soon as we are introduced to the technique and are able to reproduce satisfactory results in performing the method, we have passed from level two into level three (Conscious Competence). However, the technique will still not be a reliable method of self-protection that can be used in a violent encounter.

In a fight, you seldom have time to think, but must react. This means that even if you are able to do a technique and reproduce satisfactory results with the technique, it is still not a tool that can be relied upon in self-protection. In order for the technique to be reliable, you must have entered the fourth level of learning (Unconscious Competence). This is when you will experience "Conditioned Reflex" in your technique. This is when the technique "Does itself."

It takes time and repetition in training in order to Biuld your kung fu into a conditioned reflex. Patience is as important as talent in the learning process.

It is important that the practitioner does not attempt to force the learning process. Becoming impatient will only hinder the ability to learn. Grandmaster Ip Chun warns, "Everything in nature has its timing. When you plant a seed, you water it, give it sunlight and nurture it. As time passes you begin to see the plant grow. If you pull on the plant to help it grow, you will damage it rather than help it. The same is true of your Kung Fu training. The term Kung Fu means 'Energy and Time.' It takes both to master Wing Chun."

There is a systematic progression to Wing Chun training. The foundation is laid with the first form "Siu Lim Tao." Then the student moves on to Chum Kiu, the second form, followed by Biu Gee, the third and final hand form of Wing Chun. During the time between beginning Siu Lim Tao and the completion of Biu Gee training, the student will be taught the guiding principles, and training methods that will develop balance, coordination, sensitivity, energy development and use, as well as fighting applications.

After the empty hand forms and related training is complete, the student will be taught the Mook Yan Jong "wooden dummy form" which will help coordinate footwork, body energy, as well

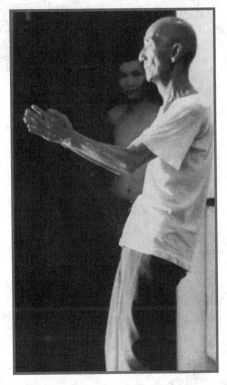

Photo taken by Ip Chun during the filming of the 8MM. Ip Ching looks on.

as defensive and counter-offensive techniques. After this the student will be taught the two weapons of the Wing Chun system, the Luk Deem Boon Kwun "Long Pole" and Bart Jam Dao "Double-Knife." Both of these teach the principles of long range and short range weapons application.

Some instructors may introduce the wooden dummy training before or simultaneously with the Biu Gee form training. The order of introduction of this training is largely one of personal preference of the instructor. However, prior to learning either the Biu Gee or wooden dummy, the foundation of Siu Lim Tao and Chum Kiu training must have been solidly laid. We must crawl before we walk, and walk before we run. To expect to progress outside of the natural process will only bring disappointment.

CHAPTER 4

Basic Principles

Wing Chun is a very practical system guided by a set of underlying principles which form the theoretical foundation of the system. A basic understanding of the following principles will help the student in their pursuit of Mastery of the Wing Chun system.

Centreline

The centreline principle is at the foundation of most Wing Chun techniques. The protection of your own centreline and the attack of the opponent's centreline are at the very heart of Wing Chun methodology.

Most of the body's vital areas lie directly on or within a few inches to either side of the centreline. This makes the protection of ones own centreline of vital importance, and attack of the opponent's centreline of strategic value.

Proper training of Siu Lim Tao level Wing Chun will build the conditioned reflex of protecting the centreline.

Theory of Facing

In the theory of facing, the Wing Chun fighter can face the opponent squarely. In Western Boxing and several other systems the fighter will have one hand/shoulder as the forward or lead side. In Wing Chun's method, the fighter can react equally with either hand and is not restricted in reach or range of motion by starting

with one side forward and the other back. Even if the Wing Chun fighter has one leg as the lead leg, the upper body can still remain square, so in Wing Chun a lead leg does not mean a lead side. The square nature of Wing Chun's facing posture makes protection of the centreline much easier and natural.

This enables the Wing Chun practitioner to spring into a leading stance on either side of the attack should they wish to, thus making Wing Chun a flexible and effective fighting system.

Gates, Doors, and Zones

Wing Chun divides the body into a matrix of areas in order to understand effective attacking and protective methods. When you look at the body as it is facing you, the centreline divides the body into two equal halves. The outside shoulder lines form the outer boundary lines. The area inside the outside shoulder lines is considered the "Indoor Area." Outside the shoulder line is considered the "Outdoor Area."

Understanding these boundary lines becomes important in applying attacks and in the understanding of proper defensive techniques. For example, if the opponent applies a straight punch, a defensive maneuver which applies a block from the "Outdoor Area" will

be much safer than one from the Indoor Area", as you will not be in immediate reach of the opponents other hand. Also, the "Outdoor Area" block has an excluding or jamming effect on the opponent's non-punching hand.

The body is also divided into upper, middle, and lower areas known as "Gates." This helps define the proper tool to use in protection of the body against attack, as well as helping in the understanding of properly directed attack. For example, Wing Chun generally keeps it's kicking attacks at, or below the waist line, which forms the upper boundary line of the "Lower Gate." It is the belief in Wing Chun that to kick above the "Lower Gate" will leave you off balance and vulnerable to attacks to your own "Lower Gate" during any kick above this target area on the opponent. Although high kicks can be powerful they leave you vulnerable, hence Wing Chun keeps its kicks low.

The remaining portion of the matrix is that of "Zones." This is the portion of the matrix that teaches about the reach of our offensive weapons and defensive tools. The area of our reach is divided into three zones. Zone one is the extreme outskirts of our reach. In attack, we can see that in this zone the opponent is outside the reach of all of our upper weapons with the exception of our fingertips. Zone one is primarily one of "Kicking Range."

In zone two the opponent will be vulnerable to your knee, punch, palm, and Fak Sao, as well as still being in range of the zone one weapons.

Zone three is for close range weapons use. Many of the attacks used in zones one and two will not be very effective at this range as it is too close to use proper structure to generate power. Techniques such as elbow and shoulder strikes will be used in this zone. The Wing Chun practitioner has a wide repertoire of different elbow strikes that can be used. These include Kop Jarn or downwards elbow strike as seen in the image above. This technique makes up a large part of Wing Chun's third form. The Wing Chun practitioner can also use Pie Jarn, which is a horizontal elbow strike developed in Chum Kiu. The power of Wing Chun elbows can be devastating.

Defensively, zones are used to explain the effective tools for blocking. In zone one, the hands and legs are used defensively.

In zone two, the forearm is the primary tool of defense through the use of Biu Sao, Bong Sao, Jaum Sao, Tan Sao, and a number of other defensive techniques.

Zone three is primarily one of trapping the opponent's hands for defense. However, techniques such as the strike Kop Jarn can also be used defensively at extremely close range to block an opponents attack. Other techniques such as Kwan Sao or rotating arms, can be use to free ones self from a trap in this zone.

The Wing Chun Guard

The hands are placed in the centreline in front of the solar plexus. This will mean the guard is never too far from a potential attack, therefore allowing efficiency of movement. If there is a gap between the hands then the centreline will

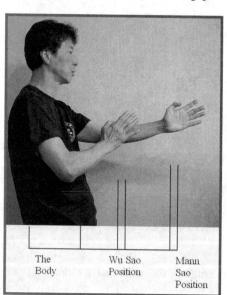

be open. This will render the principle of using the guard as a wedge useless. Furthermore, it can make you vulnerable to having your guard opened.

The Side Profile of the Wing Chun Guard

Distancing is vital. The Wu Sao (guard hand) must not be too close to the body because this will not allow room to move quickly. For example, if one wanted to perform a quick Bong Sao (wing arm) block

The Body   Wu Sao Position   Mann Sao Position

and the Wu was too close to the body, it would have to travel out before returning with the block, causing massive inefficiency and wasting important time. Also, if the Wu Sau is too close, it can be pinned to the body. If the gap between the Mann Sao (searching hand) and Wu Sao is too small, both arms can be taken out in an attack as if they were one arm. If either of the hands is pushed out too far, they lose structure and expose the practitioner to finger Chin-Na (Joint Locking) as well as to attacks to the lower rib area that was previously covered by the elbows.

The Wing Chun Punch

Wing Chun Kung Fu teaches to utilize the vertical fist instead of the horizontal fist taught in many other martial art methods. The vertical punch structure allows for better power in the punch from much shorter distances. The reason is that the shoulder is a ball & socket joint. When the arm is extended in front of the body in a punching position with the hand in a vertical attitude, the shoulder remains in its natural anatomical position. However, when the hand is rotated into a horizontal attitude, the shoulder joint moves into an unnatural position, which structurally disconnects the punch from the power source, (the body) at the shoulder. In this position the shoulder acts like a shock absorber, which robs the punch of much of its natural power.

You can test this yourself by performing the following:

Extend a hand out in front of your body in a vertical punch at shoulder level. With your other hand reach out and cup your hand around your fist and gently pull straight back towards your body against the fist. Feel the structure of the shoulder of the punching arm. In this position it should be very firm and strong.

Next rotate the punching hand to a horizontal position and do the same test. You should feel the shoulder become less firm and strong. This is due to the weakness of the shoulder in this position.

In Wing Chun's punch, the punch is locked in to a natural alignment so that the body maintains its power structure. This allows the Wing Chun fighter to generate an amazing amount of power from very short distances.

According to Grandmaster Ip Ching, "The power in the Wing Chun punch is in the last few inches."

Punching Power

It is important that the arm remains loose when throwing a punch until the last few inches before reaching the target. This is because muscle groups work in opposing ways, so when tense they prevent the punch reaching full speed. For example, the biceps pull and the triceps push, so if the arm is tense, both muscles are working against each other. This is much like driving with one foot on the accelerator and the other on the brake. This will slow the punch. It is essential that the punch reaches its full speed to be effective. This can be explained in physics by Newton's 2nd law of motion: Force equals mass multiplied by acceleration. Given that the mass of any fist providing it is tense, is constant, and unchangeable, increasing the fist's speed is the best way to increase the force of a punch. Hence remain loose for speed until nearing the target where tension should occur. The fist is also to remain loose until just before the point of impact.

When delivering a single powerful punch, use the whole body. The fist leads, and as the punch gets close to its target, you must drive the power up using your stance through the hips by rotating them toward the target, and pushing all the energy through the arm into the fist at the last moment. A common mistake many people make here is to push the hips out first, resulting in the punch being more like a push than a strike.

When striking, you must aim through or slightly past the target, but not too far or too short.

Too far will result in a push, and too short compromises power.

Chain Punching

Chain punching in Wing Chun is a very practical approach to punching as compared to other systems. In the chain punch, the hands are held in the centreline. The punch is pushed forward by the elbow. After the punch hits its target, the elbow will drop out of the punch as the next punch is launched along the same line simultaneously. As this next punch hits its target, the elbow will

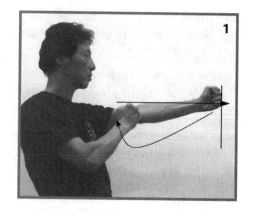

drop out of the punch and the next punch will follow in the same manner.

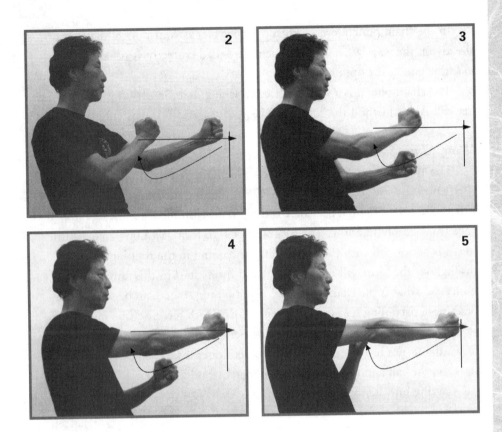

Chain punches can be thrown as two or more punches. One should aim to do about five punches a second, because this ensures a barrage of attack on the opponent, but also ensures the punches are sound. When beginners try to chain punch they should develop power and technique before speed.

The punch should always be propelled along a perfectly straight line into the target. A common mistake is to allow the punch to drop before it hits the target. This will dramatically reduce the power and damage of the punch and so should be avoided.

Another common mistake when chain punching is to not withdraw the hand back enough to get power for the next punch. When the punch is being withdrawn it should always be withdrawn to the Wu Sao position, which is the position about a fists distance from the practitioner's chest. This ensures the next punch has the distance to build power. Once the arm is withdrawn into the Wu Sao position the previously exposed ribs are covered, so it is vital to ensure the hand returns to the correct place when chain punching.

In the chain punch, even if the opponent blocks your punch, the next one is already on the way. When chain punches are used correctly, it is like firing a machine gun at the opponent.

The chain punch is a very effective attacking method in Wing Chun. Bruce Lee called this method the "Straight Blast."

Wing Chun Stances and Stepping
The Wing Chun Training Stance—Gee Kim Yeung Ma

It must be stressed that the Wing Chun training stance is not a stance in which one would fight. The stance is used to develop the leg muscles and balance from simply standing. The first Wing Chun form, Sil Lim Tao or "Little Idea", is performed with the practitioner remaining in the training stance throughout the form. All of the other hand forms start in this same training stance. So what is the training stance? The training stance can be seen as the practitioner standing feet shoulders width apart with feet pointing inward to form an imaginary triangle, the knees are bent, and the hips are pushed slightly forward, but not to the extent that the practitioner loses balance. This will put stress on the calf and other leg muscles, thereby building them.

Getting into stance or Hoi-Ma, is done by starting with the feet together. Then the knees are bent so ones feet are only just covered i.e. cannot be seen by the practitioner when looking down. The hips are then pushed out. The feet are then twisted on the heel outward so the toes are pointing to the left and right of the body At 180 degrees. Pressure is then put on the balls of the feet before the heels are rotated out from under the body. The feet should then be shoulders width or just over shoulders width apart, pointing into a position in front of the body, forming an imaginary triangle.

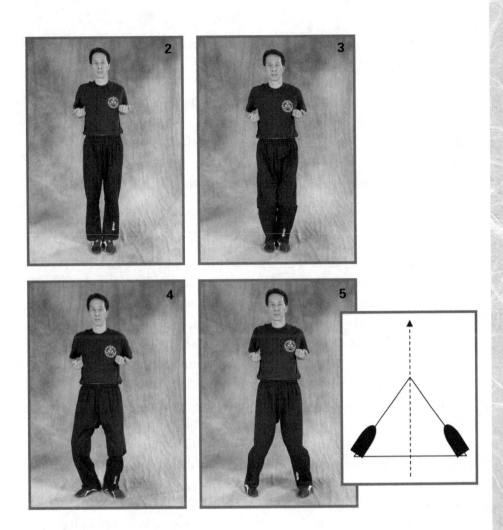

Biu Ma

Biu Ma or thrusting stance is used to refer to the kind of stance and foot-work developed in Chum Kiu. Wing Chun's stepping is designed to give its practitioner maximum stability, whilst maintaining maximum security from attack. The basic position of one's feet when using Biu Ma is as follows: Feet are approximately shoulders width apart or slightly over, and the feet are at 45 degrees. The power for the stepping comes from ankle strength built through the Achilles tendon, as well as leg strength. The power for the step is driven from the back leg. The practitioner should direct power down into the ground with the back leg, and then thrust the power out, remembering to move the front leg first. Always check the position of the feet when in place. Do not leave the feet too close together or too far apart. A common mistake is to stand on your toes, but this prevents the generation of extra power in the step, and also compromises the structure of the practitioner.

In order to give the practitioner maximum stability, whilst maintaining maximum security from attack the feet should be slightly over shoulders width apart as this gives maximum stability. Further apart and the balance is too spread and the legs become very vulnerable targets. Any closer and the legs have little balance as all your weight is balancing on a small area. Feet should be at approximately 45 degrees and parallel. If they are both square on in a forward direction, they are immobile, and if they are square on at any direction they expose the knee joint and shin area to attack. It will also inhibit the practitioner when changing direction to deal with an attack from the side or behind if the feet are square on. The knees should also be slightly bent, conforming to the Chinese martial saying which warns that "A straight leg is a broken leg." Also when the legs are bent, they are like a coiled spring ready to move. Almost all of the practitioner's weight should be on the back leg, which enables for a fast advance and retreat as one leg is thrusting forward, back or to the side. This also means weight does not have to be shifted to kick with the front leg as it can move without disrupting the balance, or telegraphing the intention to kick.

Therefore, with the weight on the back leg, front kicks can be performed easily and swiftly. Furthermore, having weight on the back leg prevents an attack to the front leg being as dangerous to your balance. This is useful because the front leg is the most likely to be attacked. The feet should be flat on the floor when stationary as opposed to being up on the toes as this gives a more stable surface on which to fight. Standing on your toes is like fighting on stilts. The feet should be flat and only push up onto the toes when pushing off during stepping. Once the step is complete, the foot must always be firmly rooted to the ground.

Huen Ma

Huen Ma or "circling stance" is the stance and footwork that is developed in the 3rd form Biu Gee. Huen Ma is extremely effective when combined with the footwork of Biu Ma. Huen Ma enables the practitioner to shift weight and change position quickly and safely.

The Huen Ma is a very flexible movement and can be used and applied in a multitude of different ways. It can be used to aggressively receive attacks or to circle around your opponent to attack them from a different angle. It can also be used to maneuver safely when fighting multiple opponents.

Two Way Energy and the Lap Sao

Two way energy sounds like a complex term. However it is simply referring to the way a Wing Chun practitioner can use their opponent's force against them. A prime example of this is when the practitioner combines a Lap Sao with a strike. The Lap Sao can be a continuation of the force of the opponent's punch; when combined with a strike like a Fak Sao the other way, the result is a greater impact.

Another way of looking at this is to imagine an object like a car moving at 30 miles an hour. If it hits an object that is standing still it will do a certain amount of damage. However, if it hits another car moving in the opposite direction, the collision and damage will be dramatically increased.

The practitioner uses the stance as a pivot point, so if for example the left side of the body performs a Lap Sao, then the stance turns away from the opponent on the left side. The result of this is that the right side of the body moves forward. This forward motion can be used to add power to the strike. One of the benefits of this kind of two direction energy is that it enables the practitioner to deliver a strike that is much more powerful than would be delivered by just the strike alone.

When using two way energy the practitioner must balance the motion so that it is one smooth movement without a stutter or stopping. This ensures that all the power is unified. A common mistake is to pull when performing the Lap Sao. This prevents two way energy as a pull places all the force in one direction. Instead, the Lap Sao should be powered by the turning in the stance. The practitioner should use the Yiu Ma or waist energy. This is difficult to master however, once the practitioner develops the generation of power coming from their stance, they will be able to Lap Sao much bigger and stronger opponents with a coordinated strike which can be devastating.

CHAPTER 5

Siu Lim Tao—Building the Weapon

The system of Wing Chun Kung Fu is comprised of three empty hand forms, Siu Lim Tao, Chum Kiu, and Biu Gee. One form on a training device called a Mook Yun Jong (Wooden Man Dummy), and two weapon sets, Luk Deem Boon Kwun (Long Pole), and Bart Jam Dao (Double Knife).

The Siu Lim Tao is the structural foundation upon which all else will be built. Without a good foundation, all that follows will be inherently weak. Without a strong Siu Lim Tao, everything else learned will be a mere shadow of the real Wing Chun.

Literally translated, Siu Lim Tao means "Little Idea." The meaning is that all learning begins with a little idea of the subject matter.

Like all of the forms taught in Wing Chun, the Siu Lim Tao is not a form used to impress audiences in demonstrations. It is a tool for developing and perfecting the students fighting ability. Wing Chun Kung Fu is not a flowery pretty system to look at. The system is designed to be efficient, economical, and practical. It is said that the Wing Chun Fighter should be "Pretty after the fight, not during the fight."

The Siu Lim Tao, unlike forms in other martial art systems, is not set up like a choreographed fight scene or dance. The form is much closer to being set up like the English alphabet. As Ip Ching once said in a lecture on Sil Lim Tao,

"When we learn English, we learn 26 letters first. If we cannot handle the pronunciation of each letter, then our English will never be good. The magnitude of the fist form Sil Lim Tao in Wing Chun is the same as that of the letters in English. If we don't master Sil Lim Tao well, we can never do well in Chum Kiu, Biu Gee, and Muk Yan Jong (Wooden Dummy)."

There are 26 letters in the English alphabet. The alphabet is set in an order for memorization, but not in an order which would dictate their use. Once the alphabet is memorized, the person has the 26 tools needed to form words. Words are then taught. The student learns the word, its proper spelling and meaning. Then the student learns to put words together to form a sentence expressing thought. Sentence order or syntax is then taught so that the student understands the proper word order and components which go into forming a proper sentence. Then sentences are put together in order to form a more complete expression of thought.

Like the above example, the Siu Lim Tao form is in an order so that the student can learn the proper hand and arm positions which form the defensive and offensive tools of the system. The form is in an order for memorization of the tools, not in a specific order which would suggest a method of application of those tools. Once the tools have been learned, the guiding principles of use are taught. The student then learns to put the separate techniques together in combination to express the desired result. So as you can see, learning Wing Chun is much like learning a physical language, complete with the freedom of expression found in the written or spoken language.

The Siu Lim Tao begins with the proper setting up of the training stance, Siu Lim Tao Ma (Ma simply meaning stance in Chinese). Here the student learns to root their body weight in such a way as to create a very stable base. Once the stance has been initially set up, there will be no further footwork or shifting. This form is done in a stationary position for two reasons:

Standing in the basic stance throughout the form will begin to train the legs to support us in our fighting stance, helping us to develop power for our techniques by Biulding a strong base.

Secondly, the stationary nature of Siu Lim Tao lets the student focus on proper hand and arm position without the added complication of stance shifting, or stepping.

Siu Lim Tao teaches the student how the blocks and attacks of Wing Chun fit within the structure of their own body. Students will be taught how each movement references specific lines and positions of their body. This allows the student to build firm and powerful defensive tools and devastating striking techniques. The training also creates "body memory" or the technique seeking the proper structural position on its own, without the students conscious thought. It is only when this body memory has been developed that one can truly depend on the technique during a violent confrontation.

According to Grandmaster Ip Chun, "The Siu Lim Tao is divided into three distinct sections, each with a purpose. The first section is for building the correct energy. Concentration is on the fingertips, thumb, wrist, and elbow. The second section is about using the energy, focusing it to the end, the last six inches, which is the way Wing Chun uses power. In Wing Chun we learn that the use of Power (Gung Lik) in a technique lasts a very short time. The power is very explosive. We relax, explode, and relax.

The third section of Siu Lim Tao is about the training of the use of the power and learning the relax, explode, relax timing for each technique."

As stated before, each technique in Siu Lim Tao has a proper positional relationship to the practitioner's own body. Grandmaster Ip Ching uses a method of training which employs a pole used as a reference. The pole is placed standing in front of the practitioner, a little beyond the reach of the punch at full extension. The pole is in line with the practitioner's centreline. On this pole there will be three reference points marked that correspond with the practitioner's body. Point one will be in line with the navel. Point two is in line with the shoulder height, or where the straight punch lines up at shoulder height. And point three is in line with the eye height. In using this method of training the practitioner learns the correct position of each of the techniques in the form. He will have a reliable reference of the centreline plane, and learn the proper height of application of each of the techniques.

Grandmaster Ip Ching reminds students that "each movement of Siu Lim Tao is driven by the elbow." So the elbow is of utmost importance in the training of this form. Movements are either pushed forward or pulled backwards by the elbow, so that is where the students mind (intent) should be in performing the movements of Siu Lim Tao."

It is also very important that the student maintains a completely straight body during the performance of Siu Lim Tao. When punching it is very easy and quite natural for the student to employ the shoulder and turn the body in the direction of the punch. But this is an incorrect method in performing Siu Lim Tao. The body remains in a square, straight forward position throughout the entire form. According to Grandmaster Ip Chun, "Since it is easy for the

beginner to move his shoulder when he should be holding his position, a mirror can be a very good training tool during the training of Siu Lim Tao. Using a mirror allows the student to see their hand position, know where their centreline is, and see if they are moving the body from its intended position."

Relaxation is one of the major keys of this training. Again, Ip Chun relates, "the expert is one who can keep his elbow in without stiffening, the muscle is still soft; elbows in, hand relaxed. This is very important for the student to master."

The Siu Lim Tao form is the building of the weapon of Wing Chun. The actual application or use of that weapon can only be taught once the weapon has been properly assembled. Just as you could not use a gun that has no firing pin and trigger, you will be unable to apply Wing Chun until you have completed development of the tools of Wing Chun through the training of the Siu Lim Tao.

Siu Lim Tao Form

1. Standing ready to start the form.

2. Master Kwok clears his mind ready to concentrate on the form

3. The hands are pulled up to chest height as closed fist. The hands do not touch or rest on the chest. This should be the case throughout the form.

4. The knees are bent.

5. Turn out on heels.

6. Turn the heels out by putting the weight on the balls of the feet. Weight is sunk to train the development of the legs and the hips are pushed slightly forward to ensure the spine remains straight. This is the training stance Gee Kim Yeung Ma. The practitioner may find it helps to imagine clamping an object between the knees as they are locked in their position. The buttocks must be tense while in this stance.

小念頭

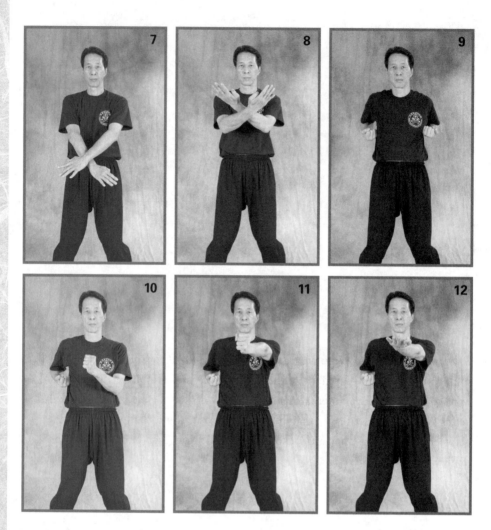

7. The hands are crossed in the centreline at the wrists. Like two crossed low Jum Sao's. The wrists are in front of the waist, This ensures the hands are not too close to the body or too far away.

8. The arms are lifted and the forearms rotate to face towards the practitioner. Like two crossed Tan Sao's.

9. Both arms are simultaneously pulled back like a double elbow strike.

10. The left fist is brought into the centre.

11. A left punch is thrown. The bottom three knuckles are used to hit so the wrist remains inline with the forearm and all the power is delivered to the end of the fist.

12. The fist is opened palm up.

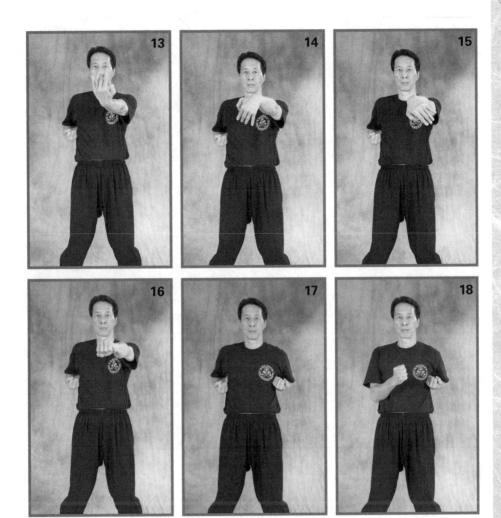

小念頭

13. The hand is folded back whilst remaining in the centreline.

14. A Huen Sao is performed circling through the inside.

15. The Huen Sao is fully circled.

16. The hand is closed into a fist.

17. The arm twists back into place through an elbow strike.

18. The right hand is placed in the centre.

19. A right punch is thrown.

20. The fist is opened.

21. The hand is folded back.

22. A Huen Sao is performed.

23. The Huen Sao is fully circled.

24. The hand is closed into a fist.

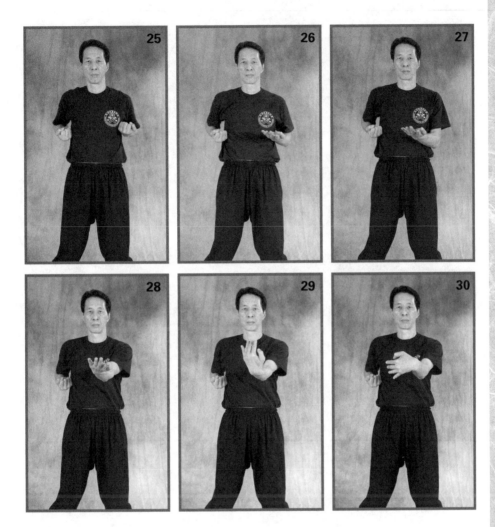

25. The arm twists back into place through an elbow strike.

26. The left palm opens.

27. Begin slowly forwarding a Tan Sao through the centreline. The key point of focus is on the thumb; by pulling the thumb back it creates tension that builds the forearm as it pulls the Tan Sao through the centreline.

28. The Tan Sao is completed.

29. The hand is folded back.

30. A Huen Sao is performed.

31. The Huen Sao continues.

32. The hand drops into Wu Sao in a small sharp Jutting motion (like Jut Sao). The Wu Sao is slowly withdrawn. The focus should be on the wrist when withdrawing the Wu Sao.

33. Once the Wu Sao is about a fists distance (3 inches) from the body, it is stopped and all energy and tension is relaxed.

34. The Wu Sao drops into a Fook Sao.

35. The Fook Sao is pushed forward. The point of focus is on the the wrist.

36. The energy and tension in the Fook Sao is relaxed and the Fook Sao is dropped into Huen Sao.

37. Once the Huen Sao is complete the hand drops into Wu Sao in a small sharp Jutting motion. The Wu Sao is slowly withdrawn. The focus should be on the wrist when withdrawing the Wu Sao.

38. Once the Wu Sao is a fists distance (3 inches) from the body it is stopped and all energy and tension is relaxed.

39. The hand drops into a Fook Sao for the second time. The focus is now on the back of the wrist as the Fook Sao comes forward.

小念頭

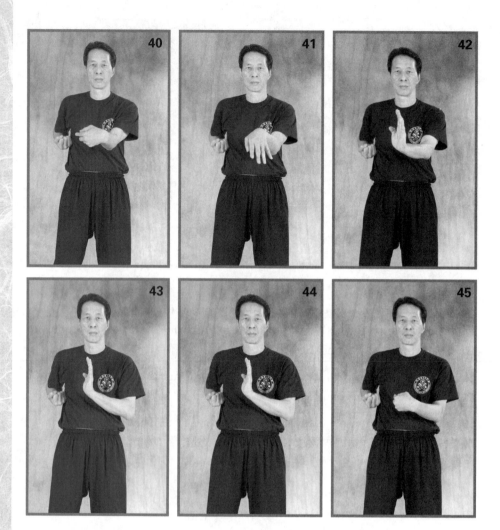

40. The Fook Sao travels through the centerline and is completed for a second time.

41. The energy and tension in the Fook Sao is relaxed and the Fook Sao is dropped into Huen Sao.

42. Once the Huen Sao is complete the hand drops into Wu Sao in a small sharp Jutting motion. The Wu Sao is slowly withdrawn. The focus should be on the wrist when withdrawing the Wu Sao.

43. The Wu Sao is withdrawn with the focus on the back of the wrist.

44. Once the Wu Sao is a fists distance (3 inches) from the body it is stopped and all energy and tension is relaxed.

45. The hand drops into a Fook Sao for the third and final time. The focus is again on the back of the wrist as the Fook Sao comes forward.

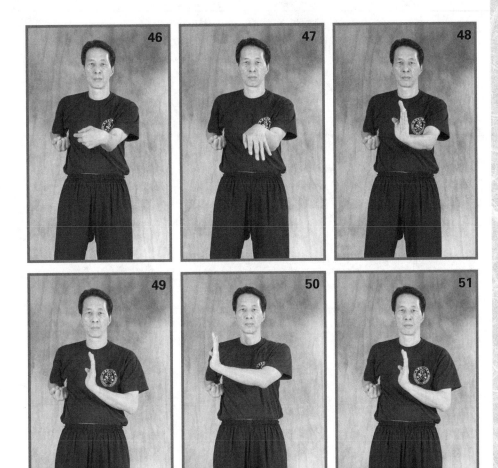

46 The Fook Sao travels through the centerline and is completed for a second time.

47. The energy and tension in the Fook Sao is relaxed and the Fook Sao is dropped into Huen Sao.

48. Once the Huen Sao is complete the hand drops into Wu Sao in a small sharp Jutting motion. The Wu Sao is slowly withdrawn.

49. Once the Wu Sao is a fists distance from the body any tension in the arm is relaxed

50. A Pak Sao is performed making sure it does not go past the right shoulder.

51. The hand comes back to the centre with the palm open and the thumb tucked in.

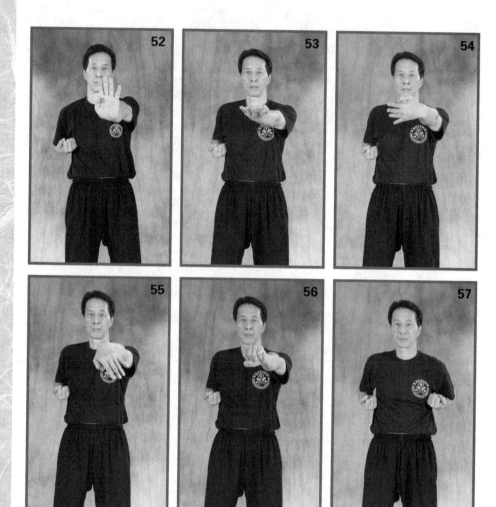

52. A vertical palm strike is performed at head height.

53. The palm rotates to face up and is fully open and relaxed.

54. The palm folds into Huen Sao.

55. The Huen Sao is performed through the inside.

56. When the Huen Sao is complete a fist is formed.

57. The fist twists back into an elbow strike.

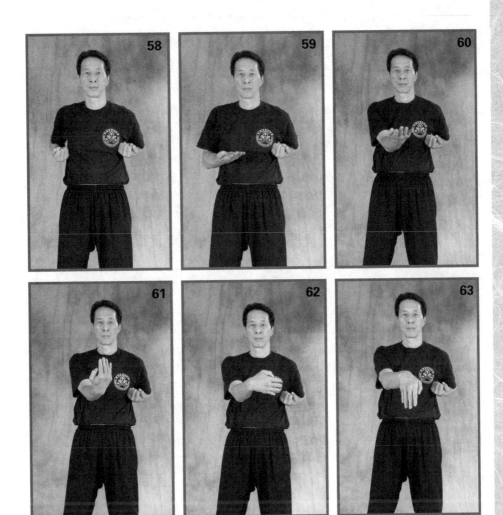

小念頭

58. The left palm opens.

59. Begin slowly forwarding a Tan Sao through the centreline. The key point of focus is on the thumb; by pulling the thumb back it creates tension that builds the forearm as it pulls the Tan Sao through the centreline.

60. The Tan Sao is completed.

61. The hand is folded back.

62. A Huen Sao is performed.

63. The Huen Sao circles round.

64. Once the Huen Sao is complete the hand drops into Wu Sao in a small sharp Jutting motion. The Wu Sao is slowly withdrawn. The focus should be on the wrist when withdrawing the Wu Sao.

65. Once the Wu Sao is a fists distance (3 inches) from the body it is stopped and all energy and tension is relaxed.

66. The Wu Sao drops into a Fook Sao.

67. The Fook Sao is pushed forward. The point of focus is on the wrist.

68. The energy and tension in the Fook Sao is relaxed and the Fook Sao is dropped into Huen Sao.

69. Once the Huen Sao is completed the hand drops into Wu Sao.

70. Once the Wu Sao is completed the energy and tension is relaxed.

71. The Wu Sao drops into a Fook Sao.

72. The Fook Sao is pushed forward for a second time. The point of focus is again on the back of the wrist.

73. The energy and tension in the Fook Sao is relaxed and the Fook Sao is dropped into Huen Sao.

74. Once the Huen Sao is completed the hand drops into Wu Sao.

75. Once the Wu Sao is completed the energy and tension is relaxed.

76. The Wu Sao drops into a Fook Sao.

77. The Fook Sao is pushed forward for a third and final time. The point of focus is again on the back of the wrist.

78. The energy and tension in the Fook Sao is relaxed and the Fook Sao is dropped into Huen Sao.

79. The Wu Sao is withdrawn.

80. Once the Wu Sao is a fists distance from the body any tension in the arm is relaxed

81. A Pak Sao is performed making sure the hand does not go past the shoulder.

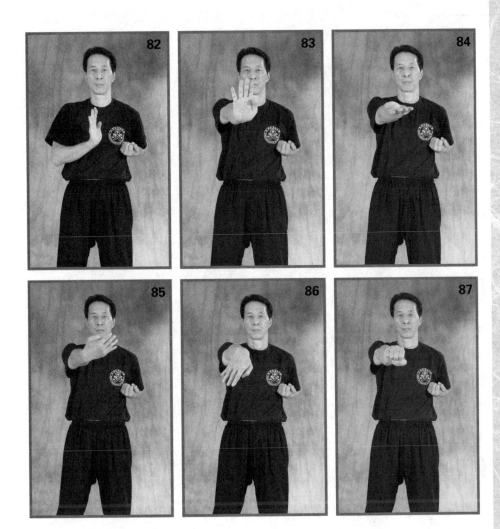

小念頭

82. The Pak Sao returns to the centre with the thumb still tucked out of the way.

83. A vertical palm strike is performed using the heel of the palm to strike at head height.

84. The palm rotates to face up and is completely relaxed.

85. A Huen Sao is performed.

86. The Huen Sao circles round.

87. The Huen Sao is completed and the fist is closed.

葉問詠春

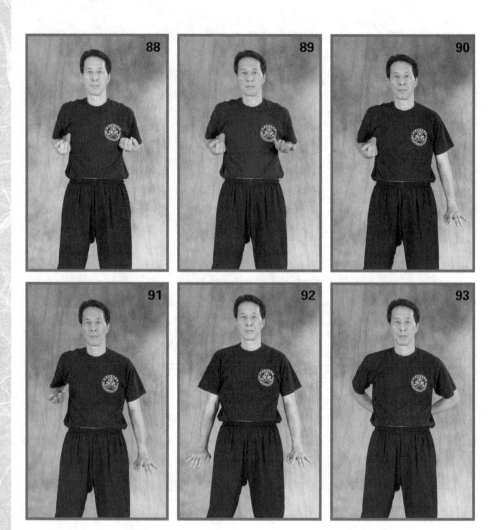

88. The arm twists back as an elbow strike. (this marks the end of the first section of Sil Lim Tao)

89. The left palm opens completely relaxed.

90. The hand travels down the side of the body completely relaxed ensuring the fingers are facing forward. Tension is applied through the last few inches of motion, after which the arms relax again.

91. The right hand opens completely relaxed.

92. The side Gum Sao is now performed on the right side.

93. The hands travel behind the body until the thumbs touch at the back.

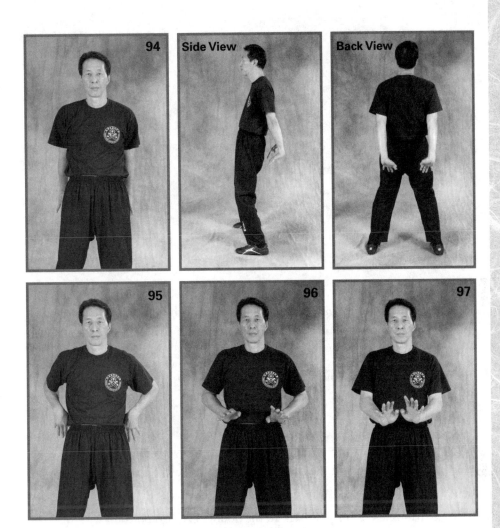

94. Both hands shoot backwards with last second energy.

95. The hands stay close to the body as they travel to the front.

96. The elbows stay bent and the arms move round.

97. The hands come to the middle completely relaxed.

98. Both hands shoot forward (not straight down) with tension in the last few inches of the Gum Sao. Notice that the hands are inline with the waist/belt level and not below.

99. The arms lift into a double Lan Sao with the left arm on top but not touching.

100. The Elbows move out first.

101. Then the hands whip out into a double Fak Sao with the knife edge of the hand tilted slightly up and the thumb tilted slightly down. The fingers tip forward very slightly to keep them from being damaged.

102. The hands and arms pull back to the double Lan Sao position with the right now on top.

103. The elbows begin to drop into the centre as the fingertips begin to point up.

小
念
頭

104. Once the arms are fully uncrossed, the double Jum Sao begins to shoot forward.

105. Last second energy and a snapping wrist action create extra force as the double Jum Sao reaches its position. The knife edge of the hand is the striking point.

106. The energy of the Jum Sao is relaxed and the palms are turned up into a double Tan Sao.

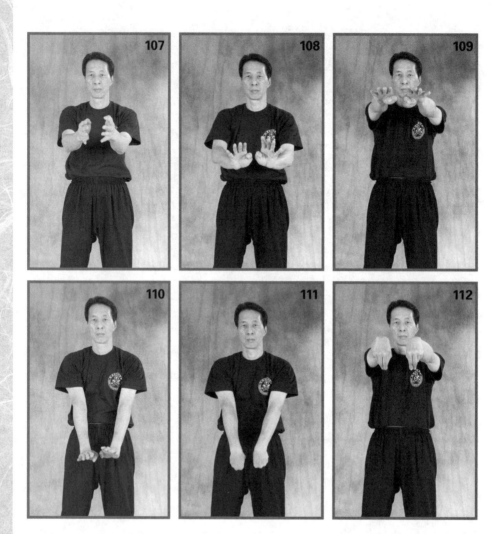

107. Tension in the forearms is created as the double Tan Sao rotates inwards.

108. A double Jut Sao is performed using last second energy.

109. The Jut Sao is fired forwards into a relaxed Biu Sao and then tension occurs at the last possible moment to ensure maximum energy is driven into the fingertips.

110. Long bridge energy is then used to drop the Biu Sao straight down without bending the elbows. A double Gum Sao is performed without tension.

111. The fingers fold back so the first finger and thumb touch.

112. The wrists are lifted without any bend in the elbow.

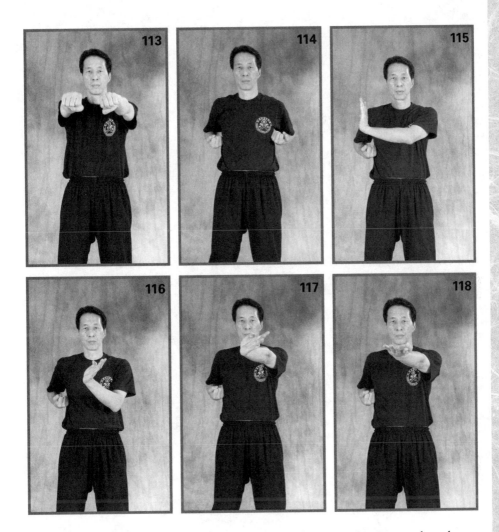

小念頭

113. An outside Huen Sao is performed. When the Huen Sao is complete the hands close.

114.Both elbows are brought back as a double elbow strike.

115. The left hand performs a Pak Sao. The hand twists into position at the last second to create additional energy. The hand does not go past the shoulder.

116. The Pak Sao is pulled back with the thumb still tucked into the edge of the hand.

117. A front knife edge palm strike is delivered at neck height.

118. The palm is rotated to face up.

119. The hand folds into Huen Sao.

120. The Huen Sao circles round.

121. The Huen Sao is completed and the fist is closed.

122. The arms are pulled back as an elbow strike.

123. The right hand performs a Pak Sao. The hand twists into position at the last second to create additional energy. The hand does not go past the shoulder.

124. The Pak Sao is pulled back with the thumb still tucked into the edge of the hand.

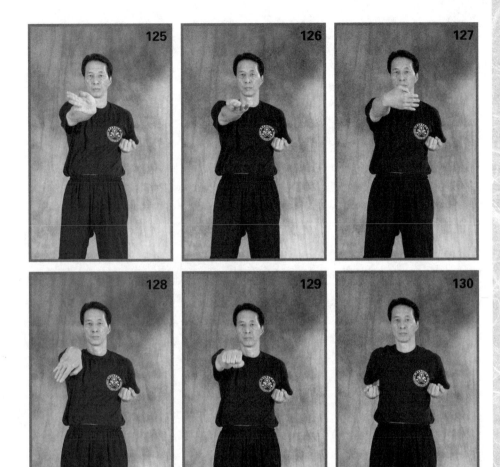

125. A front knife edge palm strike is delivered at neck height.

126. The palm is rotated to face up.

127. The hand folds into Huen Sao.

128. The Huen Sao circles round.

129. The Huen Sao is completed and the fist is closed.

130. The arm is pulled back as an elbow strike.

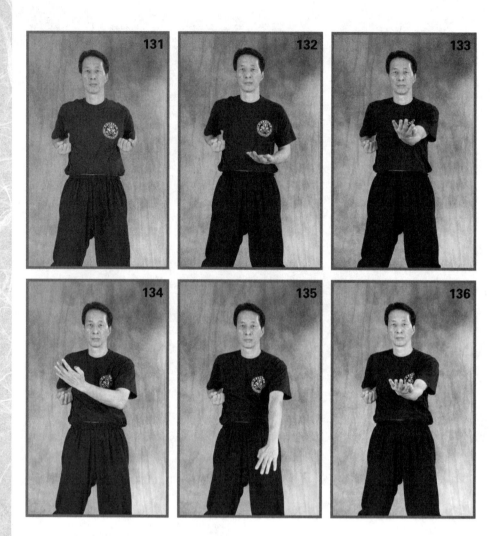

131. The left palm is then opened.

132. The left arm is pushed forward with the thumb tucked in.

133. The Tan Sao is completed with the elbow one fist distance, roughly 4 inches from the body. The elbow is not pushed into the centreline. The fingers are straight and pointing slightly up.

134. The forearm pivots around the fixed elbow position whilst the hand structure remains the same.

135. The arm drops into the low Gaun Sao position with the knife edge of the hand inline with the forearm and the fingers pointing slightly towards the centre.

136. The inside of the forearm then twists back up into a slightly lower Tan Sao. This is a different way of using the Tan Sao.

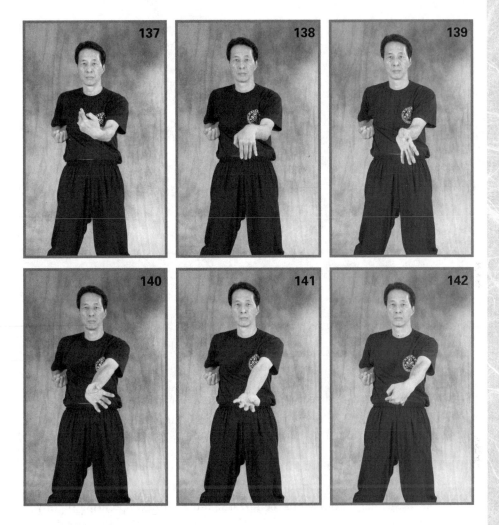

小念頭

137. The Tan Sao folds back into an inside Huen Sao.

138. The Huen Sao circles around.

139. The palm opens and begins to strike forwards into a horizontal palm strike.

140. The low horizontal palm strike is delivered to the level of the lower floating ribs. The heel of the palm is the striking area.

141. The palm is rotated and opened facing up.

142. A Huen Sao is performed.

143. The Huen Sao is completed and the fist is closed.

144. The arm is brought back as an elbow strike.

145. The right palm opens. The right arm is pushed forward with the thumb tucked in.

146. The Tan Sao is completed with the elbow one fist distance, roughly 4 inches from the body. The elbow is not pushed into the centreline. The fingers are straight and pointing slightly up.

147. The forearm pivots around the fixed elbow position whilst the hand structure remains the same. The arm drops into the low Gaun Sao position with the knife edge of the hand inline with the forearm and the fingers pointing slightly towards the centre.

148. The inside of the forearm then twists back up into a slightly lower Tan Sao. This Tan Sao uses the inside rather than the outside of the forearm.

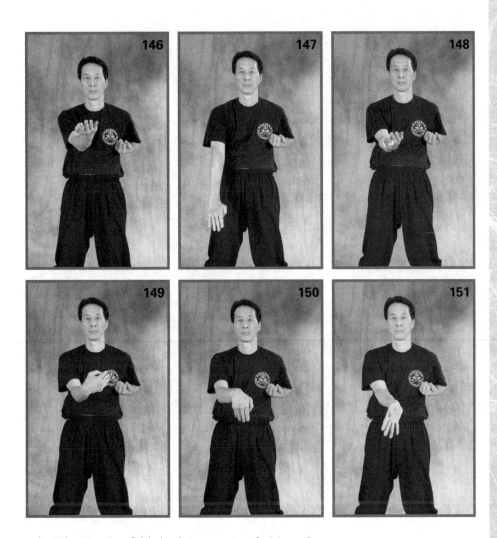

149. The Tan Sao folds back into an inside Huen Sao.

150. The Huen Sao circles around.

151. The palm opens and begins to strike forwards into a horizontal palm strike.

152. The low horizontal palm strike is delivered to the level of the lower floating ribs. The heel of the palm is the striking area.

153. The palm is rotated and opened facing up.

154. A Huen Sao is performed.

155. The Huen Sao is completed and the fist is closed.

156. The arm is brought back as an elbow strike.

157. A left Bong Sao is performed. The forearm should be rotated as the wrist is moved into the centreline where it stops. The elbow is shoulder height and the wrist is solar plexus height.

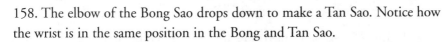

158. The elbow of the Bong Sao drops down to make a Tan Sao. Notice how the wrist is in the same position in the Bong and Tan Sao.

159. The Tan Sao is relaxed ready to deliver a heel palm strike. The thumb is kept tucked against the hand.

160. A heel palm strike is delivered to chin height with the fingers tipped back. This would be applied when attacking an opponent from the side.

161. The palm is relaxed in the face up position.

162. A Huen Sao is performed.

163. The Huen Sao is completed and the fist is closed.

葉問詠春

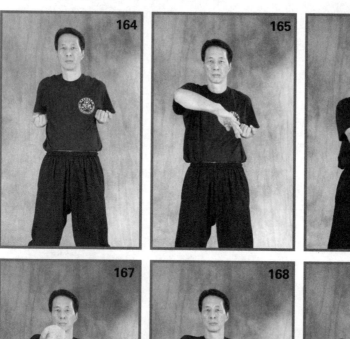

164. The arm is pulled back as an elbow strike.

165. A right Bong Sao is performed. The forearm should be rotated as the wrist is moved into the centreline where it stops. The elbow is shoulder height and the wrist is solar plexus height.

166. The elbow of the Bong Sao drops down to make a Tan Sao. Notice how the wrist is in the same position in the Bong and Tan Sao.

167. The Tan Sao is relaxed ready to deliver a heel palm strike. The thumb is kept tucked against the hand A heel palm strike is delivered to chin height with the fingers tipped back.

168. The palm is relaxed in the face up position.

169. A Huen Sao is performed.

170. The Huen Sao is completed and the fist is closed.

171. The arm is brought back as an elbow strike.

172. The left arm is brought into the centre.

173. The arm is dropped down into place like a low Gaun Sao.

174. The right hand is placed just above the elbow of the left arm.

175. The knife edge of the right hand is scraped downwards along the forearm of the left arm. This is done whilst the left arm pulls back. There should be simultaneous two way energy when performing this movement.

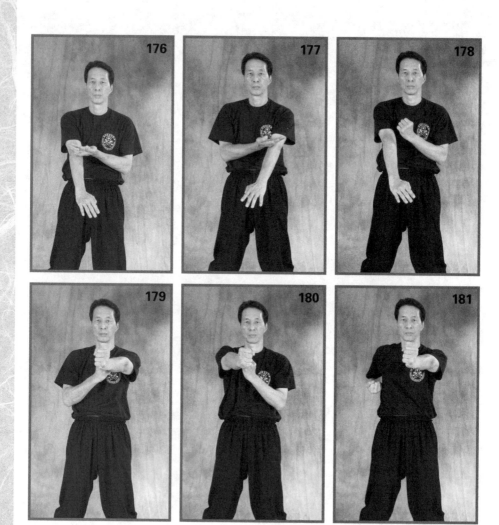

176. This results in the right hand being low and the left hand being above the right elbow. The two way energy is then performed from this side.

177. The position is once again reversed, and for the third and final time, the high hand scrapes down the forearm and the low forearm pulls back.

178. The forearm is pulled back into the centre and made into a fist.

179. The left fist performs a front punch as the right hand is pulled into the centre and made into a fist.

180. Right punch.

181. Left punch as the right is pulled back like an elbow strike.

小念頭

182. The left palm opens face up.

183. The palm folds back ready to Huen Sao.

184. The Huen Sao circles round.

185. The fist is closed.

186. The arm pulls back as an elbow strike.

187. The stance is brought together.

188. The arms begin to relax.

189. The arms drop and the body relaxes completely. Wing Chun's first form Siu Lim Tao is complete.

葉問詠春

SIU LIM TAO APPLICATIONS

小念頭

1. Master Kwok dissolves the energy of the straight punch that was thrown at him using a right Tan Sao or receiving hand.

2. A left Pak Sao is then used to control the attacking hand. The Pak Sao is kept close to the elbow to ensure maximum control of the opponent.

3. The opponent's arm is then brought down and out of the way using a Jut Sao motion which will also pull the opponent off balance. Meanwhile a finger strike to the eyes is delivered using a Biu Sao.

4. If the eye strike misses or does not do full damage, the opponent may throw a second punch. At this point, the long bridge energy that is developed in the second section of Siu Lim Tao can be used. The Biu Sao can be brought straight down without bending the elbow joint. A punch can be delivered simultaneously. In Wing Chun the blocks deflect the opponents force past the body rather than stopping it head on. This enables the practitioner to strike at the same time as blocking. When performing simultaneous blocks and strikes, turning the body can create better deflection when blocking and more power when striking. This is because the force of the turning makes the energy flow round the body from the block back into the punch.

1. The assailant grabs Master Kwok's arm in an attempt to control him and/or put him in a lock. Master Kwok ready's himself for a potential punch by bringing up his Wu Sao.

2. The assailant begins to put force on the arm in an attempt to lock it. As Master Kwok feels the force he pushes his arm down like a Gum Sao, which is performed at the start of the second section of Siu Lim Tao. Last second energy is used to ensure maximum force.

3. Master Kwok then drops his shoulder into his opponent using the force generated from the Gum Sao and from shifting his weight quickly onto the front leg.

4. As the assailant is shoulder barged away Master Kwok's hand is free and he can follow up the situation with punches if he needs to.

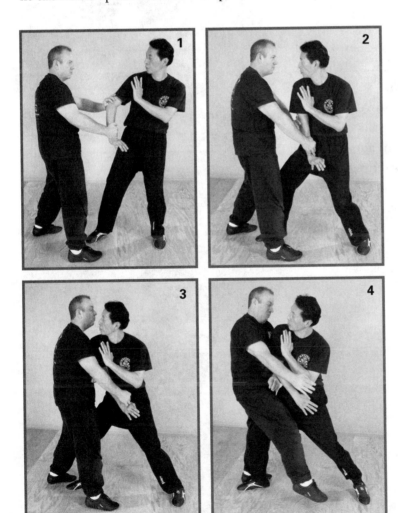

1. After being 'Bear hugged' Master Kwok moves his hands round behind himself.

2. Master Kwok suddenly drops his weight down and shoots his hands backwards into the assailant's groin. If the first strike misses or does not do sufficient damage to release the grip, Master Kwok can strike again.

1. Master Kwok blocks a traditional style punch with a Gum Sao whilst turning his stance.

2. Master Kwok then steps in slightly and delivers a straight punch of his own. The stance is turned back towards the opponent to generate extra power.

3. The punch is then pulled back ready to strike again or block if needed.

小念頭

1. Master Kwok deflects a right jab with a right Pak Sao. His Wu Sao or guarding hand is ready to strike or block.

2. The attacker throws a left cross after the jab. Master Kwok steps in and sends his guard hand forwards to cover the attack with another Pak Sao. Meanwhile the previous Pak Sao hand shoots forward as a palm strike. Master Kwok uses his step to add power to his strike.

In this photo Master Kwok blocks an uppercut style punch to his ribs using a Gaun Sao. At the same time Master Kwok delivers a knife edge palm strike to the neck.

1. Master Kwok faces his opponent with his guard up.

2. The opponent throws a punch forward and Master Kwok blocks it on the outside using a Biu Sao.

3. Master Kwok then uses a Pak Sao to remove the obstruction that is the opponent's arm. At the same time Master Kwok steps in with a front punch. Notice how the arm is only moved enough for Master Kwok to strike. If the Pak Sao is pushed any further it becomes inefficient and can send too much energy in the wrong direction, which will compromise the power of the punch.

1. Master Kwok's right forearm is grabbed.

2. The knife edge of the left hand is quickly scraped down the right arm as it is simultaneously pulled back. This uses two way energy. The previously grabbed hand is brought into the centre ready to strike.

3. A turning punch is delivered to the assailant. This can be followed up with chain punching if needed.

小
念
頭

1. Master Kwok blocks a traditional style punch using a turning Jum Sao. His Wu Sao is brought into place in case it is needed to block or strike.

2. Master Kwok then steps in with a turning punch from the right Wu Sao guard hand. The Jum Sao remains controlling the opponent.

1. Master Kwok blocks a right punch with a right Bong. This is not an ideal position to be in as a counter strike is not a viable option.

2. Therefore Master Kwok drops the elbow of his Bong Sao and turns using waist energy (Yiu Ma), he then performs a double Lap Sao. He has now thrown his attacker off balance and is now out of reach of the assailant's other hand.

3. Master Kwok then steps in with an elbow strike to the head whilst still controlling his attacker.

CHAPTER 6

Chum Kiu—Using the Weapon

In the Siu Lim Tao, the student has been introduced to the structural foundation of the Wing Chun system. The first form has taught the student the proper stance and how to root the body's weight. Each of the system's blocking hands has been introduced, and the student has learned the proper reference point at which the movement is to be aligned.

The student has learned about his centreline, the three "Seed" hands, Taun, Fook, and Bong Sao. The student has also learned how the energy is brought from the ground through the body and delivered through the elbow to the block or attack.

Through the foundation of Siu Lim Tao, the weapon has been forged. It will be in the second form, Chum Kiu, that the student will learn how to use the weapon against the opponent.

In Chum Kiu the student will learn how to develop the proper energy for application of the tools that have been developed in the Siu Lim Tao. Footwork is introduced in the second form. Stance shifting and stepping will be used to add power to the blocks and attacks that have been learned previously. Grandmaster Ip Man's youngest son, Grandmaster Ip Ching say's, "Siu Lim Tao is the most basic form of Wing Chun but Chum Kiu is the most technical." Chum Kiu is indeed the key to applying Wing Chun in combat.

Chum Kiu translated means "Seeking the Bridge." In kung fu, the bridge is the initial contact point with the opponent. There is a saying in Wing Chun that states "Attack the opponent by crossing the bridge. If there is no bridge, build one!" This saying emphasizes the importance of the bridge to the Wing Chun fighter. It is bridge contact that makes the Chi Sao (Sticking Hands) training make sense. Chi Sao is a training method unique to Wing Chun, which trains the fighter how to deal with and take advantage of the opponent when bridge contact is accomplished.

The first movement of the form is similar to the opening of Siu Lim Tao, with one very important exception. In Siu Lim Tao, the hands are crossed down and then straight up before being withdrawn. In Chum Kiu, the hands are crossed downward but then perform an inward rolling rotation being pulled through the movement by the elbows. This is the introduction to the Lap Sao or grabbing hand movement. The student will find this movement to be very useful in fighting application.

The Chum Kiu form emphasizes the Bong Sao technique. According to Grandmaster Ip Ching, "There are three seed movements in Wing Chun. The Taun Sao, Fook Sao, and Bong Sao. In the Siu Lim Tao, the Taun Sao and Fook Sao have been repeated several times, but there is only one Bong Sao in the form. In Chum Kiu, it's time to train the Bong Sao. The Siu Lim Tao has taught the student the proper structure of the Bong Sao, but it is Chum Kiu that teaches the execution of the technique with the proper power source. The Bong Sao is trained with the turning stance as well as with the Biu Ma or advancing step. The Bong Sao is even trained as a low guarding movement in the Chum Kiu. Again, according to Grandmaster Ip Ching, the number of times Bong Sao is repeated in the form shows the importance of this technique to the system of Wing Chun.

Ip Man's eldest son, Grandmaster Ip Chun explains that, "The emphasis of Chum Kiu is using both arms and both legs together, which is a difficult procedure requiring much practice." He goes on to explain, "In Siu Lim Tao you are stationary. Your movements are single hand movements. Even when you do double movements, it is for symmetry, not application. But in Chum Kiu, you are using both hands for different actions. You are changing directions and stepping in conjunction with the application of the techniques." This is what makes Chum Kiu such an important component in the Wing Chun system.

Chum Kiu also introduces kicking and elbow attacks to the Wing Chun student. Wing Chun utilizes kicking to low targets. For this reason, the kicks in the forms will usually not be performed above waist level. The kicks in the form serve a dual purpose. First and most obvious, the kicks add to our arsenal of weapons available to us in fighting. But they also help us to test the weight distribution in our stepping and shifting stance. If the student has properly stepped or shifted their stance, they should be able to apply a kick with the front leg without further shifting of the body weight.

Many Wing Chun instructors will argue over the proper weight distribution of the stance. Some will say you should have sixty percent of the weight on the rear leg, and forty percent on the front. While others say it should be a seventy to thirty percent weight distribution. Grandmaster Ip Ching simply states that, "One hundred percent of your balance should be carried on the rear leg" Notice he says one hundred percent of your balance, not one hundred percent of your weight, there is a subtle difference between the two.

By performing the kicks in the Chum Kiu form, the student will build a body memory of the proper placement of weight so that the kicks are always available to be employed without the complication of further shifting of the body weight.

Elbow attacks are also introduced in Chum Kiu. With the use of Bong Sao, the fight is often brought into extreme close range. At this range, punching is often difficult and less effective due to the close proximity to the opponent. When you find yourself too close to punch effectively, the elbow is often the best weapon of choice. In Chum Kiu the stance shifting in the first section is also training for the Por Jang or Horizontal elbow. This elbow can be utilized either to the front or pushing side of the shift or to the back or pulling side.

As you can see, the Chum Kiu has much to offer the Wing Chun student. It is truly the application form of the Wing Chun system.

Chum Kiu Form

1. Master Kwok stands ready to start the form.

2. Master Kwok clears his mind ready to concentrate on the form.

3. The hands are pulled up to chest height as closed fists. The hands do not touch or rest on the chest. This is should be the case throughout the form. The knees are bent.

4. Turn out on the heels.

5. Turn the heels out by putting the weight on the balls of the feet. Weight is sunk to train the development of the legs, and the hips are pushed slightly forward to ensure the spine remains straight.

6. The hands are crossed in the centreline at the wrists, like two crossed low Jum Sao's. The wrists are in front of the waist.

7. The forearms and hands are then folded towards the body. As this is done the elbows remain in roughly the same place. Note: This is a slightly different way to start the form compared to that seen in Sil Lim Tao. This method will train Lap Sao energy. But starting Chum Kiu either way is acceptable.

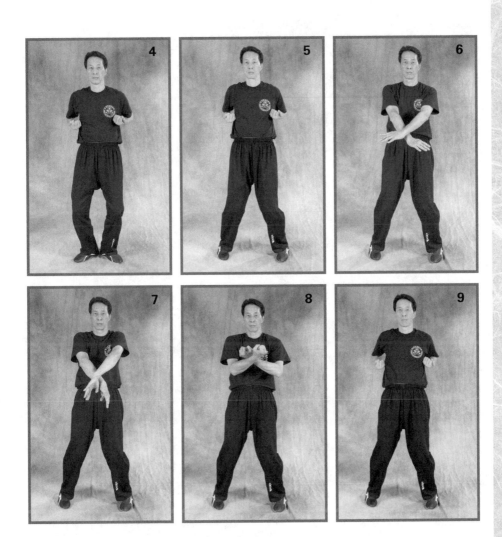

8. The arms then end up in the crossed Tan Sao position at which point the fists are closed and both hands are pulled back like a double elbow strike. Note that the hands start movement from the low crossed Jum Sao (picture 6) and finish their movement back next to the body (picture 9) the motion is not stopped in the crossed Tan Sao position as it was when performing Sil Lim Tao. The energy used for this motion should be the same as a Lap Sao

9. The arms finish their movement with the hands next to the body, but not touching the body at chest height.

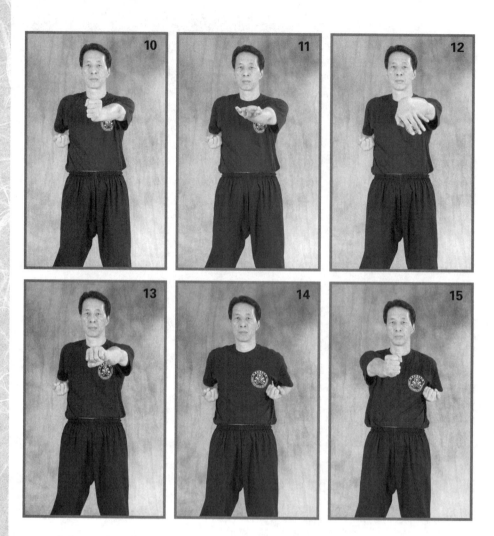

10. A left punch is thrown. The bottom three knuckles are used to hit so the wrist remains inline with the forearm and all the power is delivered to the end of the fist.

11. The fist is opened palm up.

12. The hand is folded back whilst remaining in the centreline. A Huen Sao is performed circling through the inside.

13. The Huen Sao is fully circled. The hand is closed into a fist.

14. The arm twists back into place through an elbow strike.

15. A punch is delivered through the centerline with the right hand

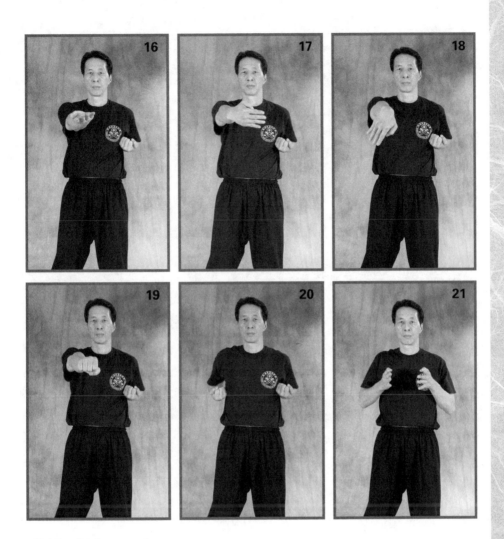

16. The fist is opened.

17. The hand is folded back. A Huen Sao is performed.

18. The Huen Sao is fully circled.

19. The hand is closed into a fist.

20. The arm is pulled back as an elbow strike.

21. The hands move towards the centre line in preparation for a double Jum Sao. The fingers are pointing forwards.

22. The hands reach the central position.

23. The hands shoot forward in a Jum Sao motion with energy focused on the knife edge of the hands. Last second energy should be used in the strike.

24. The hands fold back into a double Lan Sao position. The left arm is above the right arm and the arms do not touch. The fingertips are level with the elbows.

25. Turn to a left-facing stance whilst maintaining the double Lan Sao position. The feet and hips turn 45° whilst the head turns 90°. Focus on putting power into the elbows when turning. When turning the weight is shifted onto the back leg.

26. Turn to a right-facing stance in the double Lan Sao position. Again focus the elbows in order to gain a fast but stable turning.

27. The third turn is completed to face left.

28. The hands go forward to perform a double Fak Sao.

29. The elbows of the double Biu Sao drop into the position of a double Tan Sao. The hands are turned to face upwards and the elbows should be roughly a fist's distance from the chest.

30. The right hand is raised ready to perform a downwards Pak Sao.

尋
橋

31. The right hand is pulled down on to the left bicep to complete a downwards Pak Sao motion. As the right arm performs the downwards Pak Sao, forward energy is put into the left arm in a palm strike motion. The combination of the palm strike and downwards Pak Sao creates two way energy.

32. The right hand moves back to a Tan Sao position. The left hand is raised.

33. The left palm is pulled on to the right bicep to complete the downwards Pak Sao motion as the left hand now performs an upward heel palm strike.

34. The right arm is raised to begin a downwards Pak Sao motion as the left hand begins to return to the Tan Sao position.

35. The left arm reaches a Tan Sao position and a downwards Pak Sao motion is performed with the right arm. Once again, the left hand simultaneously palm strikes.

36. The right arm is brought back to a Wu Sao position.

37. The right arm performs a vertical palm strike as the left arm comes back to a Wu Sao position. A very slight twist in the shoulders helps generate the two way energy for these palm strikes.

38. The left arm then performs an upright palm strike, and the right arm comes back to a Wu Sao position.

39. The left hand becomes a fist and the arm is withdrawn as an elbow strike. Meanwhile the right arm performs the third and final upright palm strike.

40. The right arm is turned into a Lan Sao as the body begins turning to face the opposite direction.

41. The turn is completed with the focus on the elbow to strike, like Pie Jarn. The arm finishes in the Lan Sao position.

42. The arms relax and the left hand comes into the centre line.

43. The body turns into a left-turned stance with feet and hips at 45°. Simultaneously, a Bong Sao is performed with the right arm and the left arm goes to a Wu Sao position. The head faces in the direction of the Bong Sao. Last second energy should be put into the Wu Sao. Notice how the elbow and shoulder are in line from the front perspective.

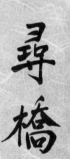

44. The body then turns to a right-facing stance. During the turn, tension is put into the right arm's wrist and elbow as the right arm becomes a Lan Sao. Simultaneously, the left hand becomes a fist and the arm is withdrawn as an elbow strike backwards.

45. The body is then turned to a left-facing stance. The right arm goes into a Bong Sao as the left arm becomes a Wu Sao.

46. Master Kwok turns to a right facing stance. During the turn the right arm becomes a Lan Sao. The left hand becomes a fist and the left arm is withdrawn as an elbow strike.

47. The body turns to a left-facing stance. The right arm goes into the third and final Bong Sao as the left arm becomes a Wu Sao.

48. The body then turns to a right facing stance. During the turn the right arm becomes a Lan Sao. The left hand becomes a fist and the left arm is withdrawn as an elbow strike.

49. The left fist moves forwards slowly to reach the right arm at the elbow of the Lan Sao.

50. When the left fist reaches the elbow on the right arm's Lan Sao, the left fist shoots forward as a punch. Simultaneously, the right arm is pulled back as an elbow strike. This requires the use of two way energy.

51. The body then turns to a forward-facing stance. Simultaneously, the left arm is extended to the left as a Fak Sao. The knife edge of the hand is the focus of energy for the Fak Sao.

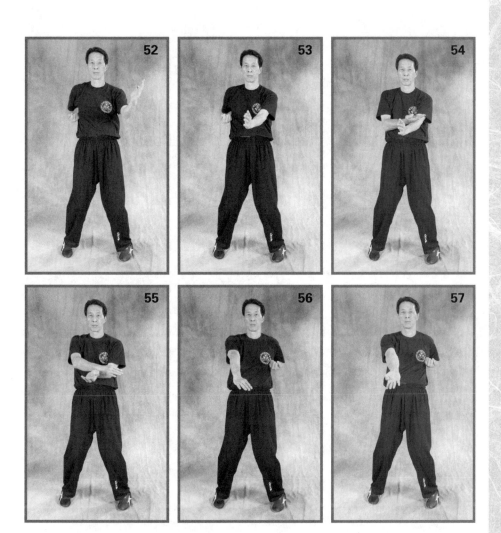

52. The left arm is brought down as a Jum Sao. The motion is led by the elbow. It is important that the elbow reaches the centreline first as this is the quickest way to recover the centreline.

53. The Jum Sao position is completed.

54. The upturned right hand is placed on the left arm.

55. The right hand is scraped forwards along the left arm. As the right hand is scraped forwards, the left hand is turned to face palm up.

56. The right arm is extended as the left hand is closed into a fist and the arm is withdrawn as an elbow strike. This should be done swiftly using two way energy.

57. The right hand is turned to face palm up.

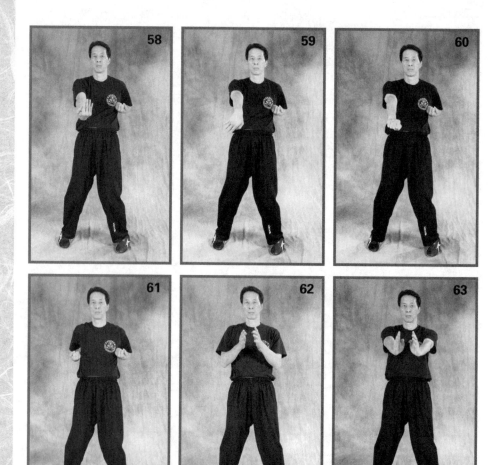

58. A Huen Sao is performed.

59. The Huen Sao is completed.

60. A fist is formed.

61. The arm is withdrawn as an elbow strike.

62. The hands come towards the centre and the fingers are pointed forwards.

63. The arms shoot forward into a double Jum Sao strike. It is the knife edge of the hands which are making the strike and where the energy is focused.

64. The body turns to a right-facing stance and the arms are brought into a double Lan Sao position.

65. The body turns to a left-facing position, remembering to focus on the elbows like before.

66. The body then completes its third and final turn to a right-facing position.

67. The arms are extended to perform double Fak Sao.

68. The arms and palms are turned upwards and the elbows are dropped as a double Tan Sao is performed.

69. The left hand is brought on to the right bicep as a downwards Pak Sao is performed with the left arm. As the left arm performs the downwards Pak Sao, forward energy is put into the right arm in a palm strike motion. The combination of the palm strike and downwards Pak Sao creates two way energy.

70. The right palm is brought on to the left bicep as a downwards Pak Sao whilst simultaneously performing a palm strike with the left palm.

71. The left hand is brought on to the right bicep as a downwards Pak Sao whilst simultaneously performing a palm strike with the right palm.

72. The left hand is brought into the centreline ready to strike.

73. The left arm performs an upright palm strike as the right arm is brought to a Wu Sao position. The slight twist in the shoulders when performing these palm strikes should help create more power through two way energy.

74. The right arm performs an upright palm strike as the left arm is brought to a Wu Sao position.

75. The left arm performs an upright palm strike as the right hand forms a fist and is brought back as an elbow strike.

76. The right arm reaches the completed elbow strike position as the left arm is relaxed ready to perform the Fak Sao.

77. The body turns to a left-facing stance with the same angles as before. Simultaneously, the left arm is brought into a Lan Sao position.

78. The body turns to a right-turned stance as a Wu Sao is performed with the right arm, remembering to use last second energy. A Bong Sao is simultaneously performed with the left arm.

79. The body then turns to a left-facing stance. Simultaneously, the left arm is brought into a Lan Sao position as the right arm is withdrawn as a backwards elbow strike.

80. The body then turns to a right-turned stance as a Wu Sao is performed with the right arm and a Bong Sao is performed with the left arm.

81. The body then turns to a left-facing stance. Simultaneously the left arm is brought into a Lan Sao position as the right arm is withdrawn as an elbow strike.

82. The body turns to a right-turned stance as a Wu Sao is performed with the right arm and a Bong Sao is performed with the left arm.

83. The body turns to a left-facing stance. Simultaneously the left arm is brought into a Lan Sao position as the right arm is withdrawn as an elbow strike.

84. The right fist is slowly brought forwards until it reaches the left arm next to the elbow.

85. Once the right fist reaches the elbow of the left Lan Sao, the right arm shoots forwards as a punch. Simultaneously, the left arm is withdrawn as an elbow strike. This uses two way energy.

86. The body then returns to a forward-facing stance. Simultaneously, the right arm is extended to the right as a Fak Sao.

87. The right arm is brought down as a Jum Sao. The motion is led by the elbow.

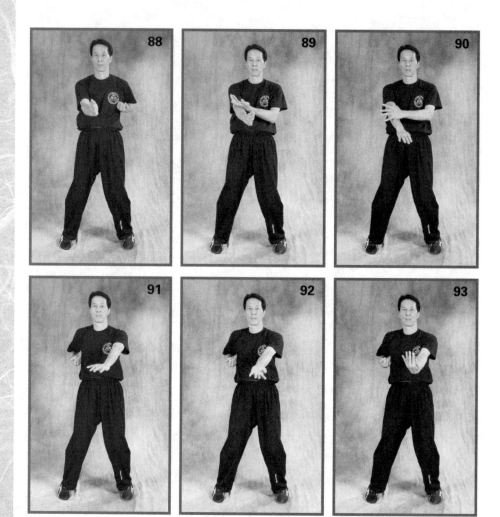

88. The Jum Sao is completed.

89. The left hand is turned palm up and is placed on the right arm.

90. The left hand is scraped forwards along the right arm.

91. The left arm is fully extended. The right hand is turned into a fist as the right arm is withdrawn as an elbow strike.

92. The left hand is turned to face palm up.

93. A Huen Sao motion is performed.

94. The Huen Sao is completed.

95. A fist is formed.

96. The arm is withdrawn as an elbow strike.

97. The left arm moves to the centre.

98. The body turns into a left-facing stance. A Lan Sau is performed as the turn is made. The power should be driven to the elbow of the Lan sau to train the Pie Jarn elbow strikes.

99. The Lan Sao position is maintained as a kick is performed with the left leg. The kick strikes with the heel of the foot. The kick is performed by lifting the heel in a straight line from the ground towards the target. The leg is not chambered before kicking forwards. It is one smooth motion.

100. The kick reaches its end position at hip height. Tension is put into the leg at the last moment to ensure the knee is not over-extended. Tension at the last moment also ensures a solid kick.

101. The left leg is brought down. When the left leg is brought down it is an advanced position, as if the left leg had taken a step forward. The right leg shifts forward to return the stance to a position where the feet are shoulder-width distance apart. Meanwhile a Bong Sau is performed with the right arm and the left arm is brought into the Wu Sao position. The head faces the direction of the Bong Sao block and not the direction of the stepping.

102. The hands are turned palm up in preparation for the next movement.

103. A thrusting step (Biu Ma) is performed to the left. Simultaneously, the right arm is brought into a Bong Sao position and the left arm is brought into a Wu Sao position.

104. The hands are turned palm up in preparation for the next movement.

105. Another step is performed to the left. Simultaneously, the right arm is brought into a Bong Sao position and the left arm is brought into a Wu Sao position.

106. The elbow begins to drop.

107. A fist is formed with the right hand.

108. The elbow reaches the side of the body as the fist is propelled into a half circle motion.

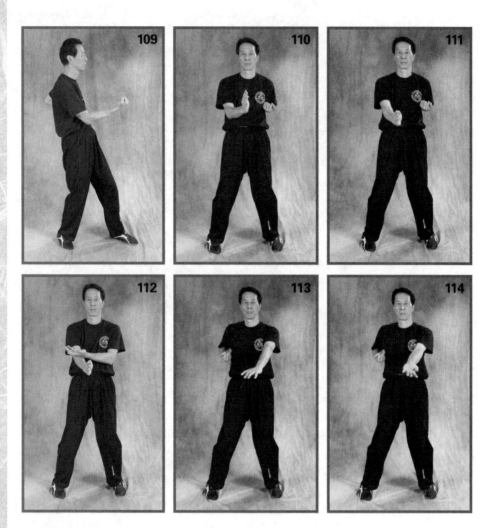

109. The half circle is complete and the punch reaches its destination

110. The body then turns to a forward-facing stance. Simultaneously the right arm performs a Jum Sao from its previous position. The elbow reaches its destination first and the hand follows to complete the Jum Sao motion.

111. The Jum Sao motion is completed.

112. The left hand is turned face up and placed on the right arm.

113. The left arm scrapes forwards along the right arm. The right arm is simultaneously withdrawn in an elbow strike.

114. The left hand is turned to face palm up.

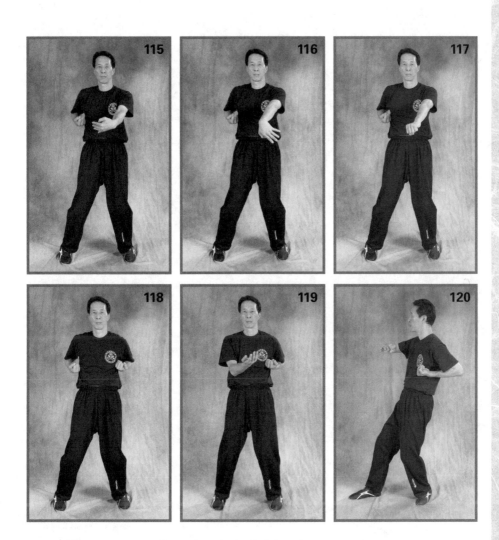

115. A Huen Sao is performed with the left hand.

116. The Huen Sao is completed.

117. A fist is formed.

118. The left arm is withdrawn as an elbow strike.

119. The right arm is brought forward for the beginning of the Lan Sao

120. The body is turned into a right-facing stance. A Lan Sao is performed as the turn is made. The energy focus is on the elbow.

尋
橋

121. The Lan Sao position is maintained as a kick is made with the right leg.

122. The kick reaches its end position at hip height.

123. The foot is brought down in an advanced position. The left foot shifts forward to return the feet to a shoulder-width sized stance. Meanwhile, the right hand is brought into the Wu Sao position as the left arm is brought into the Bong Sao position.

124. The hands are turned face up.

125. A step to the right is taken. Simultaneously the left arm goes into the Bong Sao position whilst the right arm is brought into the Wu Sao position.

126. The hands are turned palm up.

127. A step is performed to the right. Simultaneously, the left arm goes into the Bong Sao position whilst the right arm is brought into the Wu Sao position.

128. The left elbow begins to drop ready to punch.

129. The punch begins in its circular motion.

130. The punch reaches its end position.

131. The body then returns to a forward-facing stance and the left hand is brought down in a Jum Sao motion.

132. The Jum Sao is completed.

葉問詠春

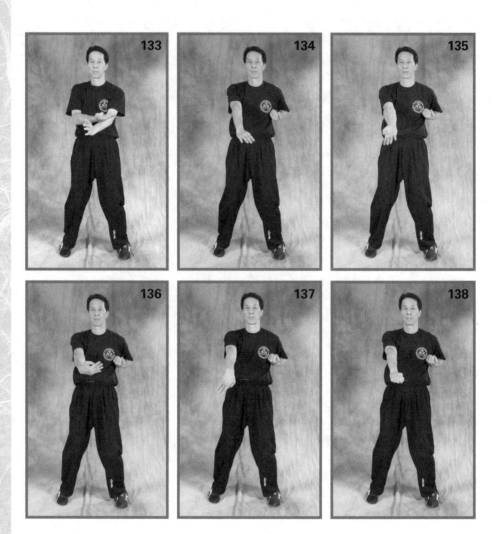

133. The right hand is turned palm-up and is placed on the left arm.

134. The right hand is scraped forwards along the left arm. Simultaneously, the left hand forms a fist and the left arm is withdrawn in an elbow strike.

135. The right palm is turned palm up.

136. A Huen Sao is performed.

137. The Huen Sao is fully circled.

138. A fist is formed.

139. The right arm is withdrawn in an elbow strike.

140. The body turns to take a left-facing stance.

141. A kick is made with the left leg.

142. The left leg is brought down in an advanced position. The right leg shifts forwards to return the feet to a shoulder-width stance. Simultaneously, the arms are thrust forwards and downwards into a double low-Bong Sao position. This stepping is used to jam up an opponents attack and is called Big Ma.

143. The arms are turned into a double Tan Sao position.

144. Another Big Ma step is taken forwards. The arms are thrust forwards and downwards to perform a double low-Bong Sao.

葉問詠春

145. The arms are turned into a double Tan Sao position.

146. Another step is taken forwards. For the third and final time, the arms are thrust forwards and downwards to perform a double low-Bong Sao.

147. The arms are turned into a double Tan Sao position.

148. A double Huen Sao motion is performed as the weight is shifted forwards on to the left foot.

149. Once the Huen Sao motion is completed, a double Jut Sao position is taken in preparation to perform a Jut Sao motion. Simultaneously, the right foot comes forward to take a position next to the left leg.

150. Once the right foot reaches the left foot the knees bend as the weight is sunk. Simultaneously, a double Jut Sao motion is made.

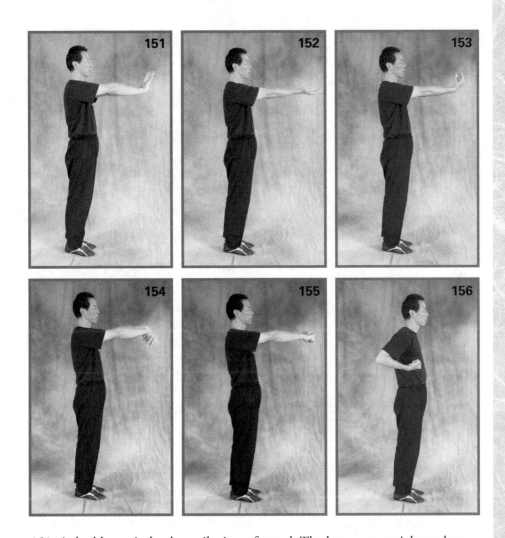

151. A double vertical palm strike is performed. The knees are straightened as the strike is made, which adds power.

152. The hands are turned palms up.

153. A double Huen Sao is performed.

154. The double Huen Sao is completed.

155. Two fists are formed.

156. The arms are withdrawn as a double elbow strike.

尋
橋

157. The right foot is moved backwards and placed shoulder width distance from the left foot.

158. Once the right foot is placed on the ground, a turn is made so that a right-facing stance is taken. The weight is placed on the back leg once again.

159. A kick is made with the right leg.

160. The right leg is brought down in an advanced position. The left leg shifts forwards to return the feet to a shoulder-width stance. Simultaneously, the arms are thrust forwards and downwards to perform a double low-Bong Sao.

161. The arms are brought into a double Tan Sao position.

162. Another Big Ma jamming style step is taken forwards. Simultaneously, the hands are thrust forwards and downwards to perform a double low-Bong Sao.

163. The arms are brought into a double Tan Sao position.

164. Another step is taken forwards. Simultaneously, the hands are thrust forwards and downwards to perform a double low-Bong Sao.

165. The arms are brought into a double Tan Sao position.

尋
橋

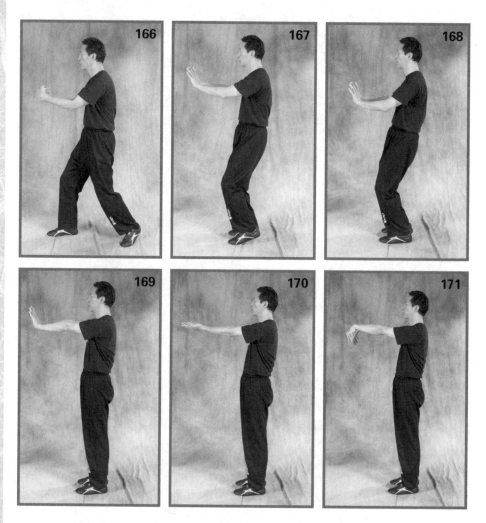

166. A double Huen Sao motion is performed as the weight is shifted forwards on to the right leg.

167. Once the Huen Sao motion is completed, a double Jut Sao position is taken in preparation to perform a Jut Sao motion. Simultaneously, the left foot comes forward to take a position next to the right foot.

168. Once the left foot reaches the right foot the knees bend as the weight is sunk. Simultaneously, a double Jut Sao motion is made.

169. A double vertical palm strike is performed. The knees are straightened as the strike is made, which adds power.

170. The hands are turned palms up.

171. A double Huen Sao is performed.

172. Two fists are formed.

173. The arms are withdrawn as a double elbow strike.

174. From this position, a kick is aimed at hip height approximately 135° to the left. To perform this kick, the weight is transferred onto the right leg, and the right foot is turned inwards. As with previous kicks in the form, the left heel is driven directly towards the target area and is not chambered.

175. The left heel moves towards the target area.

176. The kick continues.

177. Tension is applied to add power to the kick just before it reaches its target.

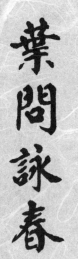

178. The kick reaches its full extension.

179. Upon the foot returning to the floor, the body immediately shifts to a right-turned stance. To achieve this, once the kick reaches its extended position, the left foot is brought down to shoulder-width distance from the right foot. On the way down, the foot is turned 45° to the left. Simultaneously, a left Gum Sao is performed. The right hand is brought up to a Wu Sao position.

180. The body then turns to a left-turned stance and a Gum Sao is performed with the right hand. Simultaneously, the left hand is brought up to a Wu Sao position.

181. The body then turns to a right-turned stance and a third and final Gum Sao is performed with the left hand. Simultaneously, the right hand is closed into a fist and the right arm is withdrawn ready to perform a turning punch, which will regain the centreline.

182. The body then turns to a neutral stance. Simultaneously, the left hand returns to a Wu Sao position as a turning punch is thrown with the right hand.

183. A left punch then begins the chain punches that end the form.

184. Right punch.

185. Left punch.

186. A right punch is performed as the left arm is withdrawn as an elbow strike.

尋
橋

187. The right hand is opened and turned to face palm up. A Huen Sao is performed.

188. The Huen Sao continues

189. The Huen Sao is completed.

190. A fist is formed

191. The right arm is withdrawn as an elbow strike.

192. The feet are brought together, and the body completely relaxes.

193. The arms are dropped to the sides and the form is completed.

CHUM KIU APPLICATIONS

尋
橋

1. Master Kwok Catches the first punch with a downwards Jut Sao like motion using his left hand. With his right hand he applies a sudden Tok Sao type motion to the back of the attackers arm damaging the elbow joint.

2. The attacker pulls his damaged right arm away and attacks with his left arm. Master Kwok simply repeats the technique this time using his right to Jut down as his left jar's into the back of his attackers elbow.

1. Master Kwok deflects the punch with a turning Bong Sao from his right hand. The Wu Sao is brought up as an extra failsafe in case the Bong Sao is not perfect.

2. The attacker try's to force his punch through Master Kwok's defence. In response Master Kwok brings his Wu Sao hand into contact with the punch and begins to collapse his bong Sao

3. Master Kwok performs a Lap Sao from his guard hand and delivers a Fak Sao throat chop with the Bong Sao hand.

1. Master Kwok faces his opponent with his guard up.

2. The second Master Kwok notices movement from the attackers hand he quickly steps in and jams the attack with his Bong Sao, even if the attacker fakes the attack the arm can still be jammed. This skill is developed from practicing Chun Kiu. It is know as Big Ma. Notice how Master Kwok keeps his guard hand or Wu Sao up.

3. Master Kwok begins to turn the Bong Sao of to the side where his guard hand is waiting to perform a Lap Sao.

4. Master Kwok Lap's the attacking hand and delivers a punch to his opponents head. This uses two direction energy. Also notice how Master Kwok is on the outside of the attacker thus rendering the attackers other hand essentially useless for blocking or attacking.

5. Master Kwok then takes a further step around his opponent and uses his punching hand to grab the head while he delivers an elbow strike known as Pie Jarn or hacking elbows, the power for which is developed in Chum Kiu.

尋橋

1. Master Kwok jams a traditional style punch using his Big Ma that is developed in Chun Kiu.

2. As the punch is pushed forwards master Kwok turns it away from his body

3. Master Kwok is ready with his Wu Sao.

尋
橋

4. As the punch is forced further forward master Kwok begins to collapse his Bong Sao ready to perform a Lap Sao and Fak Sao strike.

5. Master Kwok Lap's with his right hand and delivers a Fak Sao with his left.

6. Master Kwok then uses Faan Sao skills developed from Chi Sao and swiftly drops the Fak Sao into a Gum Sao or pinning hand whilst simultaneously delivering a spade hand strike to his opponents face.

7. Master Kwok continues stepping with the strike to put extra force into. This uses power drawn from the feet all the way through the body into the strike.

1. The attacker applies pressure onto Master Kwok's arm. In response Master Kwok drops into a Lan Sao or bar arm position and gives some resistance to the force.

2. As a result of the resistance the attacker pushes harder on the Lan Sao, at which point Master Kwok turns his body and performs a Lap Sao from his Lan Sao. This throws the opponents force off to the side, past Master Kwok's body. Meanwhile Master Kwok delivers a punch to his assailants head. Master Kwok uses the force generated from the Lap Sao to add power to his punch.

1. Master Kwok is on the outside gate.

2. Master Kwok performs a double Jut Sao which causes a sudden jerking motion which throws his opponent off balance.

3. Master Kwok then springs forward with a double Biu Sao strike to the neck of his opponent.

4. Master Kwok pushes force through his whole body into the attack by springing forwards.

尋
橋

1. Master Kwok faces his attacker with his guard up.

2. When the punch is thrown Master Kwok shoots the heel of his foot along a straight line into the side of his attacker whilst covering the punch with a Lan Sao.

1. Master Kwok faces his opponent.

2. The opponent try's to circle round Master Kwok and attack from the side. Master Kwok responds by pivoting on his back left foot and shooting a kick towards his attacker.

3. The kick should be aimed at the attackers groin or midriff. Master Kwok also delivers a palm strike while kicking.

尋橋

CHAPTER 7

Biu Gee—Perfecting the Weapon

Biu Gee is the third and final empty hand form taught in the Ip Man Wing Chun system. It literally means "thrusting fingers." There is an old saying among the Ip Family system instructors that states, "Biu Gee does not go out the door." This means that Biu Gee was kept as a very secretive form that was only taught to a few select students who had proved themselves worthy of the training. According to Grandmaster Ip Ching, "it is essential to have a thorough understanding of proper positioning and use of force in Siu Lim Tao, and gain some mastery of the stepping footwork and stance turning in Chum Kiu, with the ability to divert the opponent's power, and make use of the opponents force to counter attack him, prior to beginning Biu Gee training." This according to Ip Ching is the real reason that not too many people learned this form from his father Grandmaster Ip Man. Many did not have the discipline and patience to develop to the stage where they were ready to undertake the Biu Gee training. It is for this reason rather than unwillingness on the part of Ip Man to teach that accounts for the lack of widespread understanding of Biu Gee.

In Siu Lim Tao we have built a solid weapon with strong structure based on body alignment and an understanding of our own bodies' natural strengths and weaknesses. In Chum Kiu, we have learned how to use stepping, shifting, and turning to create power in the use of the weapons forged in the first form. Now in Biu Gee, we learn to perfect the use of power we have developed in the other forms. This two-direction energy is perfected by Biu Gee. This energy is explosive and dangerous.

In the Biu Gee form, the student will be introduced to new footwork such as Huen Ma (Circle Stepping), as well as new elbow attacks, and the technique for which the form is named, the thrusting fingers.

Biu Gee also introduces the student to the concept of what is known as Gow Gup Sao "first aid hands" or emergency techniques. Generally the Wing Chun fighter tries to keep the opponent in a centreline facing position. When the opponent successfully flanks the Wing Chun fighter, or when an attack is launched by someone whose approach is from the side or back, then Biu Gee techniques are the ones the Wing Chun fighter will utilize in order to create or regain a superior position from which to defeat the attacker.

It is a fact that very few students ever learned this form from Grandmaster Ip Man. Grandmasters Ip Chun and Ip Ching have worked very hard to see that this form and its related training methods and principles are not lost to future generations. Grandmaster Ip Ching demonstrated this form in 1999 at the First World Wing Chun Conference in Hong Kong. His demonstration was nothing short of spectacular and showed very clearly the explosive power that training in this form can generate.

Grandmaster Ip Chun says that, "Biu Gee focuses the energy to the hand and fingertips." He further states that, "in order to develop the proper energy the student must be dedicated. Biu Gee must be practiced hundreds of times to develop this power, and hundreds more times to master the power."

In Biu Gee the student will train the Yiu Ma (Waist Energy) as the power of the movements. Movements like the double Gaun Sao, Huen Sao / Jum Sao, and double Lap Sao, will be performed with the Yiu Ma. These movements have been introduced in the earlier form training, but in Biu Gee the movements will reach a power maturity that is very impressive.

Grandmaster Ip Ching teaches that, "Every movement must be done with maximum power and speed. Movements should also be performed with a broken rhythm. Many movements in the form are done in sets of three, such as the Biu Gee movements. These should be done with a 1—2, 3 rhythm. This develops the Faan Sao or "Returning Hand" principle.

In this method the first attack is launched, and when the opponent defends the attack, we divert his power and launch a second and third attack almost simultaneously."

The Yiu Ma combined with relaxed two-direction energy can develop very explosive power. To train with someone who has gained a high degree of mastery of the power of Biu Gee is impressive.

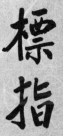

Biu Gee Form

1. Master Kwok clears his mind ready to concentrate on the form.

2. The hands are pulled up to chest height as closed fist. The hands do not touch or rest on the chest. This is should be the case throughout the form. The knees are bent.

3. Turn out on heels.

4. Turn the heels out but putting the weight on the ball of the feet. Weight is sunk to train the development of the legs and the hips are push slightly forward to ensure the spine remains straight.

5. The hands shoot forward as two crossed low Jum Sao. The wrists are crossed in the centreline.

6. The hands are pulled in towards the body. This involves pushing the elbows out very slightly. This will cause the shoulders to lift slightly.

7. As the forearms roll over the hands are closed into a fist and pulled back sharply in a Lap Sao like motion.

8. The Lap Sao motion results in the elbows being pulled back like a double backward elbow strike.

9. A left punch is delivered along the centreline. Power and tension should be put into the punch in the last few inches of its travel.

標指

10. The fingers shoot forward out of the fist.

11. The fingers are then thrust down as power is driven to the fingertips by shooting tension down the arm. The wrist will rise slightly when performing this movement.

12. The wrist is then suddenly dropped. The focus in this movement should be to try and develop power by tensing ant the last possible moment.

13. The fingers are then thrust down for a second time and once again power is driven to the fingertips by shooting tension down the arm. The wrist will rise slightly when performing this movement.

14. The wrist is then suddenly dropped again. The focus in this movement should be to try and develop power by tensing ant the last possible moment.

15. The fingers are then thrust down for the third and final time and once again power is driven to the fingertips by shooting tension down the arm. The wrist will rise slightly when performing this movement.

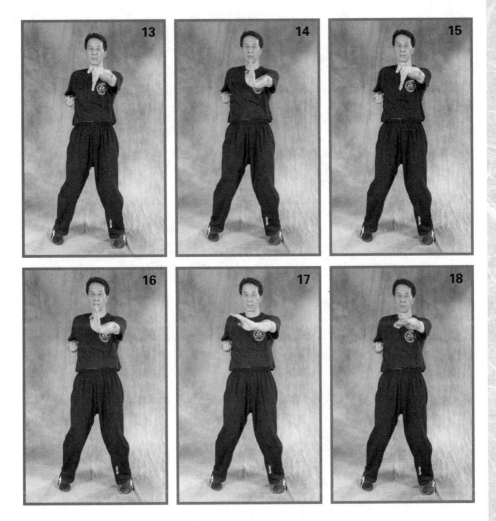

16. The wrist is then suddenly dropped for the third and final time. The focus in this movement should be to try and develop power by tensing ant the last possible moment.

17. The fingers the twist onto a horizontal plain (as opposed to their previously vertical plain).

18. The fingers of the left hand are then thrust out to the left. The focus is once again to drive power into the fingertips by use of tension at last possible moment.

標指

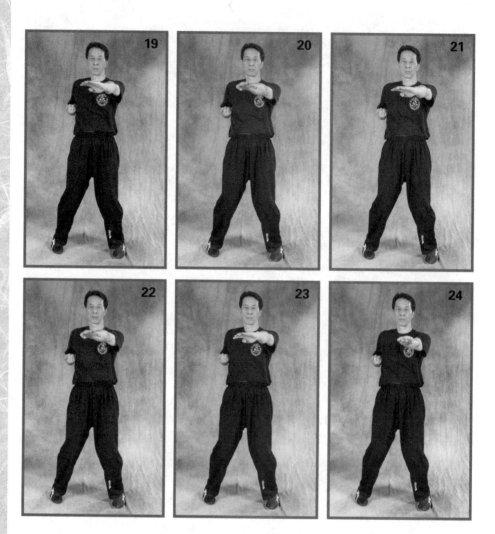

19. The knife edge of the hand is then pushed forward once again using last second energy.

20. The hand is pulled back across the centerline in a short but sharp Jut Sao motion.

21. The knife edge of the hand is then pushed forward for a second time once again using last second energy.

22. The hand is then once again pulled back across the centerline in a short but sharp Jut Sao motion.

23. The knife edge of the hand is then pushed forward for a third and final time once again using last second energy.

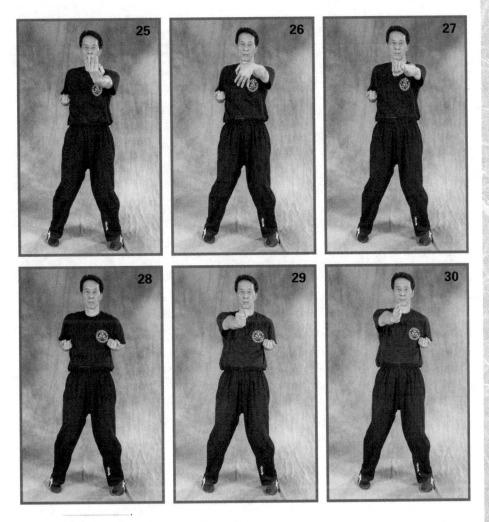

24. The hand is then turned to face palm up.

25. The hand is then folded back to perform a Huen Sao

26. The Huen Sao circles through the centreline.

27. The Huen Sao is completed and closed into a fist.

28. The fist is pulled back as an elbow strike.

29. A right front punch is delivered. Power and tension should be put into the punch in the last few inches of its travel.

30. The fingers shoot forward out of the fist.

標指

31. The fingers are then thrust down as power is driven to the fingertips by shooting tension down the arm. The wrist will rise slightly when performing this movement.

32. The wrist is then suddenly dropped. The focus in this movement should be to try and develop power by tensing ant the last possible moment.

33. The fingers are then thrust down for a second time and once again power is driven to the fingertips by shooting tension down the arm. The wrist will rise slightly when performing this movement.

34. The wrist is then suddenly dropped again. The focus in this movement should be to try and develop power by tensing at the last possible moment.

35. The fingers are then thrust down for the third and final time and once again power is driven to the fingertips by shooting tension down the arm. The wrist will rise slightly when performing this movement.

36. The wrist is then suddenly dropped for the third and final time. The focus in this movement should be to try and develop power by tensing ant the last possible moment.

37. The fingers the twist onto a horizontal plain (as opposed to their previously vertical plain).

38. The fingers of the left hand are then thrust out to the left. The focus is once again to drive power into the fingertips by use of tension at last possible moment.

39. The knife edge of the hand is then pushed forward once again using last second energy.

標指

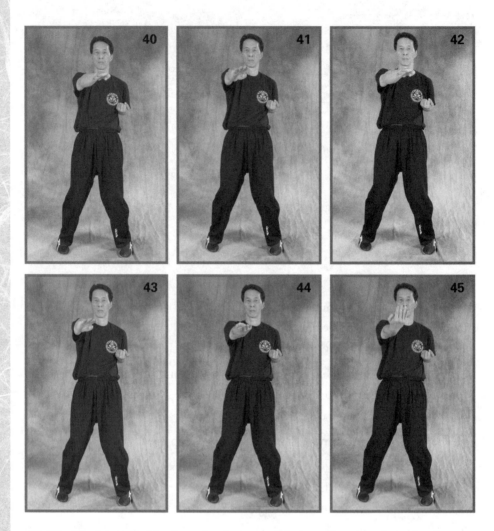

40. The hand is pulled back across the centerline in a short but sharp Jut Sao motion.

41. The knife edge of the hand is then pushed forward for a second time once again using last second energy.

42. The hand is then once again pulled back across the centerline in a short but sharp Jut Sao motion.

43. The knife edge of the hand is then pushed forward for a third and final time once again using last second energy.

44. The hand is then turned to face palm up.

45. The hand is then folded back to perform a Huen Sao

46. The Huen Sao circles through the centreline.

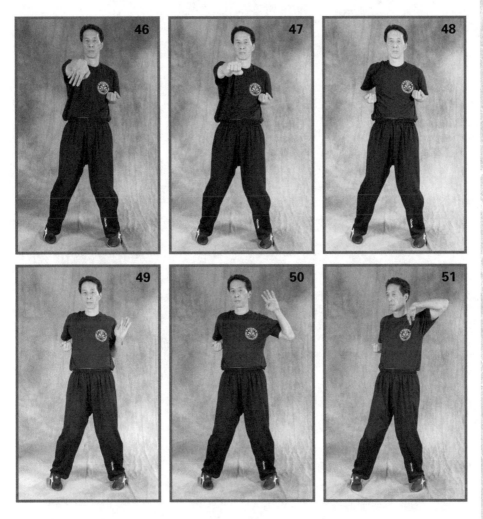

47. The Huen Sao is completed and closed into a fist.

48. The fist is pulled back as an elbow strike.

49. The left hand is opened and begins to lift.

50. The hand is pushed towards the head causing the elbow to move away from the body. This is the start of the motion called Kop Jarn or downward elbow. This technique features predominantly in the third form. The technique should be performed fast with the focus being on the elbow.

51. Once the hand is parallel to the ear the wrist is bent and the hand is folded. The hand is pushed down towards the chest as the elbow is lifted into the air. At this point the body begins to turn to the right. The turn should be used to put power into the elbow this making its striking potential more deadly.

標指

葉問詠春

52. The elbow arc's past the head of the practitioner (this covers the head from any potential attack) and then comes crashing down. The elbow should be in line with the shoulder (90 degrees from the body) and slightly lower than the shoulder (to ensure maximum power) and it should not be pushed into the centreline as this destroys the structure of the practitioner. The motion Kop Jarn is now completed.

53. The left arm then begins to pull back as the right arm pushes forward to perform the technique Kop Jarn.

54. The right hand is folded in and the right elbow rises as the left arm is being pulled back and the body begins to turn to the right. This motion should be completed using speed and power.

55. The right Kop Jarn is completed and once again the elbow is inline with the shoulder (but slightly below shoulder height) not in the centreline.

56. The right arm then begins to pull back as the left arm pushes forward to perform the technique Kop Jarn.

57. The left hand is folded in and the left elbow rises as the right arm is being pulled back and the body begins to turn to the left. This motion should be completed using speed and power.

58. The third and final Kop Jarn is completed and once again the elbow is inline with the shoulder not in the centreline.

59. The right hand is brought under the left elbow with the palm open and facing down.

60. The right hand shoots forward performing a Biu Sao motion. It is important that the hand comes from the left side of the elbow so it will successfully free the practitioner from having their elbow pinned. The left arm is simultaneously withdrawn from the Kop Jarn position to perform a backwards elbow strike. This motion should use the same energy as a Lap Sao. The fingers of the right hand will finish at throat height.

標指

61. The left hand is brought forward palm down and placed under the right elbow.

62. The left hand the shoots forward as a Biu Sao (or Biu Gee: Note Biu Sao translates thrusting hand and Biu Gee translates thrusting fingers) the power for this motion starts at the feet and is driven through the body to the finger tips. As the left hand shoots forward the left foot is also brought forward.

63. The fingertips of each hand finish next to each other. The feet are also directly next to each other.

64. Both hands are turned to face palm up.

65. A double Huen Sao is performed.

66. The hands are closed into fists.

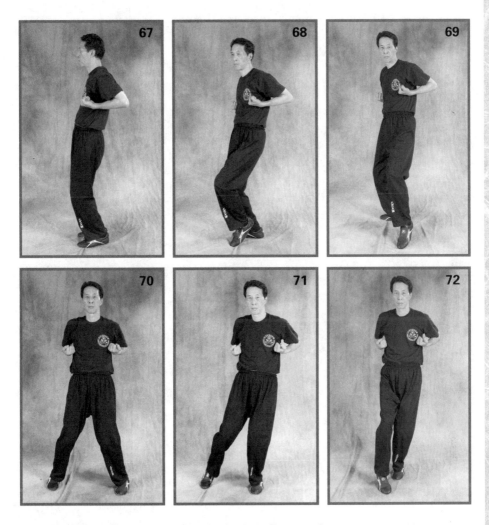

67. The hands are withdrawn like a double elbow strike.

68. The feet begin the Huen Ma motion. The left foot begins to circle out away from the body

69. A half circle motion is performed with the practitioners heal off the floor.

70. The foot is placed down just past the shoulder. And the right foot begins to lift.

71. The right foot comes all the way towards the left foot and just before it touches it is pushed out in front to perform a half circle motion.

72. The half circle is performed with the right foot.

標指

葉問詠春

73. The right foot returns to its position in stance and the Huen Ma is completed.

74. The Right hand is opened and begins to lift.

75. The hand is pushed towards the head causing the elbow to move away from the body. This is the start of the motion called Kop Jarn or downward elbow. This technique features predominantly in the third form. The technique should be performed fast with the focus being on the elbow.

76. Once the hand is parallel to the ear the wrist is bent and the hand is folded. The hand is pushed down towards the chest as the elbow is lifted into the air. At this point the body begins to turn to the Left. The turn should be used to put power into the elbow this making its striking potential more deadly.

The elbow arc's past the head of the practitioner (this covers the head from any potential attack) and then comes crashing down. The elbow should be in line with the shoulder (90 degrees from the body) and slightly lower than the shoulder (to ensure maximum power) and it should not be pushed into the centreline as this destroys the structure of the practitioner. The motion Kop Jarn is now completed.

77. The Right arm then begins to pull back as the Left arm pushes forward to perform the technique Kop Jarn.

78. The Left hand is folded in and the Left elbow rises as the Right arm is being pulled back and the body begins to turn to the Left. This motion should be completed using speed and power.

79. The Left Kop Jarn is completed and once again the elbow is inline with the shoulder (but slightly below shoulder height) not in the centreline.

80. The Left arm then begins to pull back as the Right arm pushes forward to perform the technique Kop Jarn.

81. The Right hand is folded in and the Right elbow rises as the Left arm is being pulled back and the body begins to turn to the Right. This motion should be completed using speed and power.

標指

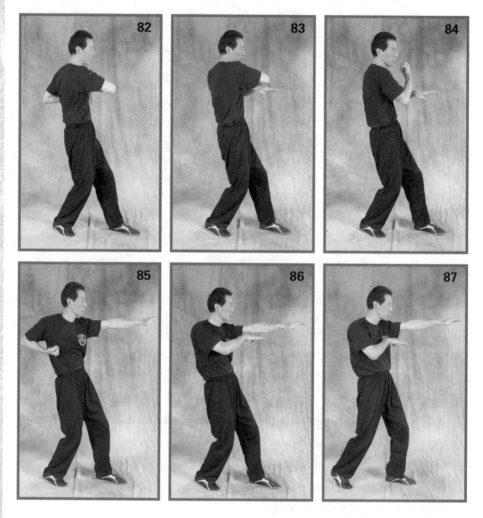

82. The third and final Kop Jarn is completed and once again the elbow is inline with the shoulder not in the centreline.

83. The Left hand is brought under the Right elbow with the palm open and facing down.

84 & 85 The Left hand shoots forward performing a Biu Sao motion. It is important that the hand comes from the Right side of the elbow so it will successfully free the practitioner from having their elbow pinned. The Right arm is simultaneously withdrawn from the Kop Jarn position to perform a backwards elbow strike. This motion should use the same energy as a Lap Sao. The fingers of the Left hand will finish at throat height.

86. The Right hand is brought forward palm down and placed under the Left elbow.

87. The Right hand the shoots forward as a Biu Sao (or Biu Gee: Note Biu Sao translates thrusting hand and Biu Gee translates thrusting fingers) the power for this motion starts at the feet and is driven through the body to the finger tips. As the Right hand shoots forward the Right foot is also brought forward.

88. The fingertips of each hand finish next to each other. The feet are also directly next to each other.

89. Both hands are turned to face palm up.

90. A double Huen Sao is performed.

標指

91. The hands are closed into fists.

92. The hands are withdrawn like a double elbow strike.

93. The feet begin the Huen Ma motion. The Right foot begins to circle out away from the body.

94. A half circle motion is performed with the practitioners heal off the floor.

95. The foot is placed down just past the shoulder. And the Left foot begins to lift.

96. The Left foot comes all the way towards the Right foot and just before it touches it is pushed out in front to perform a half circle motion.

97. The half circle is performed with the Left foot.

98. The Left foot returns to its position in stance and the Huen Ma is completed.

99. The left hand begins to lift.

100. A left Kop Jarn is performed whilst turning to the right.

101. The right hand is placed palm down under the left elbow.

102. The right hands shoots forward as a Biu Sao and the left hand is lapped back.

標指

103. The left hand is placed under the right elbow and then trusted forwards. The left foot also moves up to put power into this motion.

104. Double inside Huen Sao.

105. The hands are closed into fists.

106. The hands are withdrawn as a double elbow strike.

107. The feet begin the Huen Ma motion. The left foot begins to circle out away from the body.

108. A half circle motion is performed with the practitioners heal off the floor.

109. The foot is placed down just past the shoulder. And the right foot begins to lift.

110. The right foot comes all the way towards the left foot and just before it touches it is pushed out in front to perform a half circle motion.

111. The half circle is performed with the right foot.

112. The right foot returns to its position in stance and the Huen Ma is completed.

113. The Right hand begins to lift.

114. A Right Kop Jarn is performed whilst turning to the Left.

115. The Left hand is placed palm down under the Right elbow.

116. The Left hands shoots forward as a Biu Sao and the Right hand is lapped back.

117–119. The Right hand is placed under the Left elbow and then trusted forwards. The Right foot also moves up to put power into this motion.

120. Both hands turn to a palm up position.

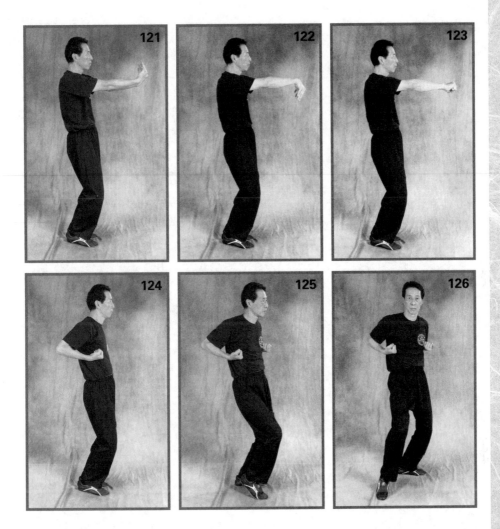

121–122. Double Huen Sao.

123. The hands are closed into fists.

124. The hands are withdrawn as a double elbow strike.

125. The feet begin the Huen Ma motion. The Right foot begins to circle out away from the body.

126. A half circle motion is performed with the practitioners heal off the floor.

標指

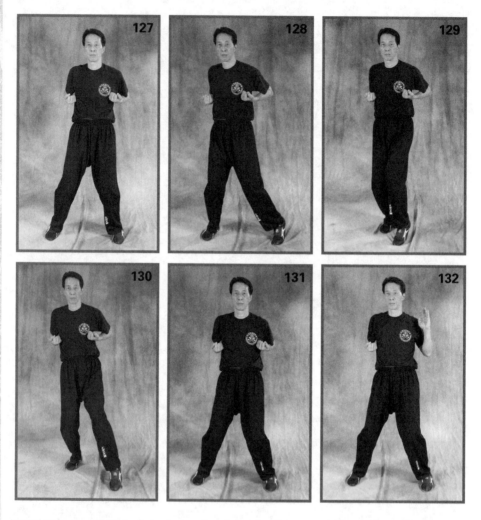

127. The foot is placed down just past the shoulder. And the Left foot begins to lift.

128–129. The Left foot comes all the way towards the Right foot and just before it touches it is pushed out in front to perform a half circle motion.

130. The half circle is performed with the Left foot.

131. The Left foot returns to its position in stance and the Huen Ma is completed.

132. The left hand begins to lift.

133. The wrist is folded as the elbow rises to perform the Kop Jarn movement.

134. The body is in a right facing stance with the left arm having completed the Kop Jarn.

135. The right hand moves under the left elbow. Again the hand is slightly to the left of the elbow approximately 1-2 inches to the left i.e. closer to the shoulder than the wrist. This is important if the practitioner is to successfully escape the elbow being pinned.

136. The right hand thrusts forward in a Biu Sao motion.

137. The right hand then begins to lap back as the left hand moves forward.

138. Two direction energy must be used at this point. This is done by turning the left side of the body forward with the strike as the right side comes back with the right Lap Sao motion.

139. The left hand then finishes as a high palm strike to jaw level. Yiu Ma should be used to add power to the strike from the hips by turning them towards the strike.

140. The left hand is whisked to the right as the stance turns back to face forward. The elbow should lead the Fak Sao motion to ensure it travels the quickest possible route. This is very important as it also ensures a larger area is covered with the motion making it a safer way to intercept any attacks from the side.

141. The edge of the hand should be angled slightly up and the thumb angled down with the fingers straight and tilted slightly forward.

142. The left hand then performs a Fook Sao to the front. Once again the elbow must lead this motion.

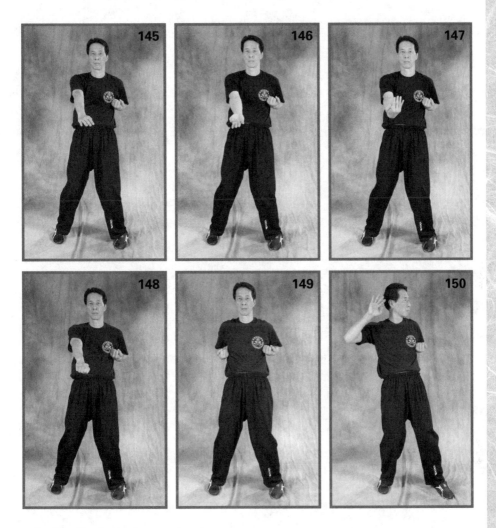

143. The Fook Sao is completed.

144. The right hand is brought up to touch the Fook Sao arm.

145. The right hand shoots forward in a clearing motion as the left hand is pulled back like a backwards elbow strike.

146. The motion is completed and the hand is turned to face palm up.

147. The hand is folded back and a Huen Sao begins to turn inwards.

148. The Huen Sao is completed and the fist is closed.

149. The arm is pulled back like a backwards elbow strike.

150. The Right hand begins to lift.

標指

151. The wrist is folded as the elbow rises to perform the Kop Jarn movement.

152. The body is in a Left facing stance with the Right arm having completed the Kop Jarn.

153. The Left hand moves under the Right elbow. Again the hand is slightly to the Right of the elbow approximately 1-2 inches to the Right i.e. closer to the shoulder than the wrist. This is important if the practitioner is to successfully escape the elbow being pinned.

154. The Left hand thrusts forward in a Biu Sao motion.

155. The Left hand then begins to lap back as the Right hand moves forward. Two direction energy must be used at this point. This is done by turning the Right side of the body forward with the strike as the Left side comes back with the Left Lap Sao motion.

156. The Right hand then finishes as a high palm strike to jaw level. Yiu Ma should be used to add power to the strike from the hips by turning them towards the strike.

157. The Right hand is whisked to the Left as the stance turns back to face forward. The elbow should lead the Fak Sao motion to ensure it travels the quickest possible route. This is very important as it also ensures a larger area is covered with the motion making it a safer way to intercept any attacks from the side.

158. The edge of the hand should be angled slightly up and the thumb angled down with the fingers straight and tilted slightly forward.

159. The Right hand then performs a Fook Sao to the front. Once again the elbow must lead this motion.

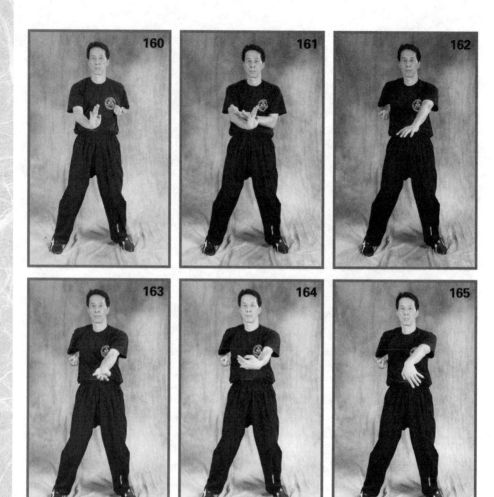

葉問詠春

160. The Fook Sao is completed.

161. The Left hand is brought up to touch the Fook Sao arm.

162. The Left hand shoots forward in a clearing motion as the Right hand is pulled back like a backwards elbow strike.

163. The motion is completed and the hand is turned to face palm up.

164. The hand is folded back and a Huen Sao begins to turn inwards.

165–166 The Huen Sao is completed and the fist is closed.

167. The arm is pulled back like a backwards elbow strike.

168. The left hand moves up past the ear as the Kop Jarn motion begins.

169. The elbow is lifted.

170. The elbow is driven down to complete the Kop Jarn motion.

171. The right hand is placed palm down under the left elbow in the same way as earlier in the form.

標
指

172. The right hand shoots forward as a Biu Sao as the left is pulled back. As always in Biu Gee the force is driven all the way to the fingertips.

173. Two direction energy and hip power Yiu Ma is used to deliver a low palm strike with the left hand as the right hand is simultaneously pulled back.

174. The edge of the hand is twisted out and the fingers are straightened in line with the forearm as a Fak Sao is delivered from the low right side to high on the left side. The Fak Sao should move swiftly and smoothly to cover the largest range of areas of potential attack.

175. Last second energy should be put into the Fak Sao as it reaches its destination as if it were striking a target. This can be done by tilting the hand and fingers slightly forward before impact. The start of the Biu Gee form trains this use of energy.

176. The hand is then dropped into the centre elbow first.

177. The Fook Sao is now complete. Notice how the fingers are always straight when performing techniques in the form. This helps keep a strong structure for striking and defending.

178. The right hand is place palm up on the left arm.

179. As the right hand shoots forward it is turned face down and the left hand is simultaneously pulled back.

180. The hand is turned palm up and begins to Huen Sao inwards.

標指

181. The Huen Sao circles.

182. The fist is closed.

183. The arm is pulled back like a backwards elbow strike.

184. The Right hand moves up past the ear as the Kop Jarn motion begins.

185. The elbow is lifted.

186. The elbow is driven down to complete the Kop Jarn motion.

187. The Left hand is placed palm down under the Right elbow in the same way as earlier in the form.

188. The Left hand shoots forward as a Biu Sao as the Right is pulled back. As always in Biu Gee the force is driven all the way to the fingertips.

189. Two direction energy and hip power Yiu Ma is used to deliver a low palm strike with the Right hand as the Left hand is simultaneously pulled back.

190. The edge of the hand is twisted out and the fingers are straightened in line with the forearm as a Fak Sao is delivered from the low Left side to high on the Right side. The Fak Sao should move swiftly and smoothly to cover the largest range of areas of potential attack.

191. Last second energy should be put into the Fak Sao as it reaches its destination as if it were striking a target. This can be done by tilting the hand and fingers slightly forward before impact. The start of the Biu Gee form trains this use of energy.

192. The hand is then dropped into the centre elbow first.

標指

葉問詠春

193. The Fook Sao is now complete. Notice how the fingers are always straight when performing techniques in the form. This helps keep a strong structure for striking and defending.

194. The Left hand is place palm up on the Right arm.

195. As the Left hand shoots forward it is turned face down and the Right hand is simultaneously pulled back.

196. The hand is turned palm up and begins to Huen Sao inwards.

197. The Huen Sao circles.

198. The fist is closed.

199. The arm is pulled back like a backwards elbow strike.

200. The right hand rises away from the body ready to cut down into a low Gaun Sao. The left hand also moves away from the body to perform a high Gaun Sao motion.

201. The right hand cuts down into a low Gaun Sao with the fingers straight and the thumb tucked in. Yiu Ma is use with the turning to make the techniques more efficient. Meanwhile the right hand is rotated up and across so that the inside of the forearm twists into place. The fingers are straight and the thumb is tucked in. The body is now facing 45 degrees to the right.

標指

202. The high left arm then hinges at the elbow to swing inside the right arms elbow so that the fingers of the left hand come close to the inside of the right arms elbow. The right arm withdraws slightly as it lifts.

203. Yiu Ma is then used to turn 45 degrees to the left as the arms swing through all potential areas of attack for the front of the body.

204. The high and low Gaun Sao is now completed with the left arm at the bottom this time.

205. The left arm is withdrawn and begins to lift as the right arm hinges at the elbow.

206. The body begins to turn to the right using Yiu Ma to assist the efficiency of the hand techniques.

207. The high and low Gaun Sao now faces right with the right hand below the left.

208. The left hand is Lapped back as the body turns to face forward and the right hand performs a small three-quarter circular Fook Sao motion that regains the centreline.

209. The Fook Sao is complete with the fingers pointing directly up with the left hand now next to (but no touching) the body.

210. The left hand now comes forward to be placed palm up on the right arm.

211. The left arm turns over to face palm down as it shoots forward and the right arm is withdraw like a backwards elbow strike. This uses two direction energy.

212. The hand is turned over and begins to Huen Sao inside.

213. The Huen Sao circles round.

214. The hand is closed into a fist.

215. The hand is pulled sharply back like a backwards elbow strike.

216. The Left hand rises away from the body ready to cut down into a low Gaun Sao. The Right hand also moves away from the body to perform a high Gaun Sao motion. The Left hand cuts down into a low Gaun Sao with the fin-

gers straight and the thumb tucked in. Yiu Ma is use with the turning to make the techniques more efficient. Meanwhile the Left hand is rotated up and across so that the inside of the forearm twists into place. The fingers are straight and the thumb is tucked in. The body is now facing 45 degrees to the Left.

217. The high Right arm then hinges at the elbow to swing inside the Left arms elbow so that the fingers of the Right hand come close to the inside of the Left arms elbow. The Left arm withdraws slightly as it lifts. Yiu Ma is then used to turn 45 degrees to the Right as the arms swing through all potential areas of attack for the front of the body. The high and low Gaun Sao is now completed with the Right arm at the bottom this time.

218. The Right arm is withdrawn and begins to lift as the Left arm hinges at the elbow. The body begins to turn to the Left using Yiu Ma to assist the efficiency of the hand techniques. The high and low Gaun Sao now faces Left with the Left hand below the Right.

219. The Right hand is Lapped back as the body turns to face forward and the Left hand performs a small three-quarter circular Fook Sao motion that regains the centreline.

標指

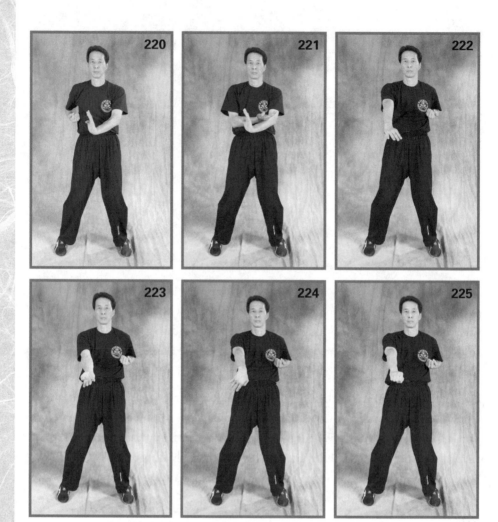

220. The Fook Sao is complete with the fingers pointing directly up with the Right hand now next to (but no touching) the body.

221. The Right hand now comes forward to be placed palm up on the Left arm.

222. The Right arm turns over to face palm down as it shoots forward and the Left arm is withdraw like a backwards elbow strike. This uses two direction energy.

223. The hand is turned over and begins to Huen Sao inside.

224. The Huen Sao circles round.

225. The hand is closed into a fist.

226. The hand is pulled sharply back like a backwards elbow strike.

227. The hands come away from the body so that the left hand comes to the low right side of the body.

228. The left hand shoots from low to high in a Fak Sao (this technique may also be referred to a Mann Sao or asking/inquisitive hand) motion. Energy is put into the motion just before impact. The fingers should be tilted slightly forward and downward so that the outside edge of the hand leads. The hand should not be flat horizontally. Meanwhile the right hand performs a Pak Sao to finish next to the left shoulder.

標指

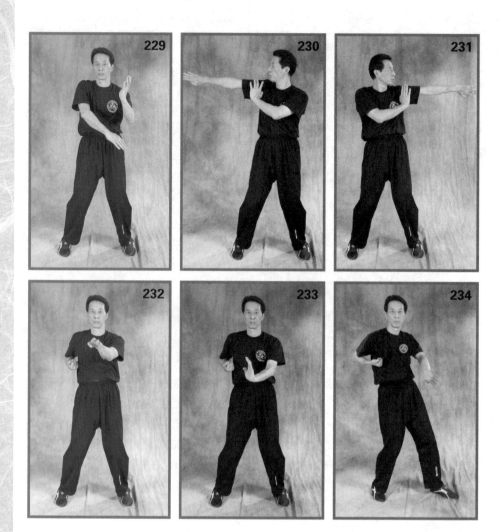

229. The right hand drops down out of the Pak Sao position so it can sweep through all the angles with the Fak Sao motion. The left hand begins to come back across.

230. The right hand completes its Fak Sao motion to the right as the left ends in the Pak Sao position next to the right shoulder ensuring it does not go past the shoulder.

231. A Fak Sao and Pak Sao is performed to the left side in the same manner as before..

232. The right hand is pulled back as the left hand moves straight across into the centreline with the base of the thumb leading the motion (rather than the elbow as before).

233. The wrist then drops performing a Jut Sao motion.

234. Yiu Ma turning is then used in conjunction with a larger non static Huen Sao motion. The hand is folded so the fingers point down as the hips are use to turn the body to the left. The hand then lifts up as the body turns back to face forward.

235. A Fook Sao motion using last moment energy finishes the circle of the Huen Sao as the hand returns to the centreline.

236. The hand cuts down then across using the power of the hips for a second time.

237. The hand finishes the second Huen Sao motion in the same way as before with a Fook Sao into the centre.

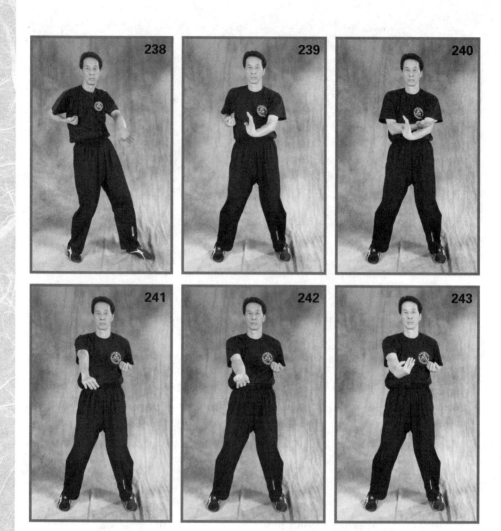

238. A third turning Huen Sao begins.

239. And is again is again finished with a Fook Sao motion back into the centre line.

240. The right hand is placed on the left arm.

241. The arm is cleared using two direction energy.

242. The right palm is turned over.

243. The hand is folded back and begins to Huen Sao.

244. The Huen Sao circles round through the inside.

245. The hand is closed into a fist.

246. The hand is pulled back like a backwards elbow strike.

247. The Right hand shoots from low to high in a Fak Sao (this technique may also be referred to a Mann Sao or asking/inquisitive hand) motion. Energy is put into the motion just before impact. The fingers should be tilted slightly forward and downward so that the outside edge of the hand leads. The hand should not be flat horizontally. Meanwhile the Left hand performs a Pak Sao to finish next to the Right shoulder.

248. The Left hand completes its Fak Sao motion to the Left as the Right ends in the Pak Sao position next to the Left shoulder ensuring it does not go past the shoulder.

249. A Fak Sao and Pak Sao is performed to the Right side in the same manner as before.

標指

250. The Left hand is pulled back as the Right hand moves straight across into the centreline with the base of the thumb leading the motion (rather than the elbow as before).

251. The wrist then drops performing a Fook Sao motion.

252. Yiu Ma turning is then used in conjunction with a larger non static Huen Sao motion. The hand is folded so the fingers point down as the hips are use to turn the body to the Right. The hand then lifts up as the body turns back to face forward.

253. A Fook Sao motion using last moment energy finishes the circle of the Huen Sao as the hand returns to the centreline.

254. The hand cuts down then across using the power of the hips for a second time.

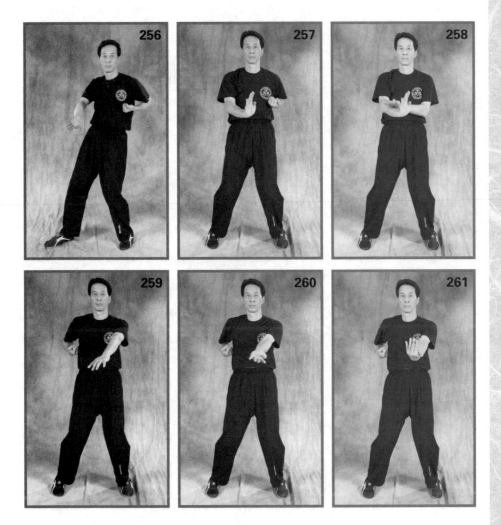

255. The hand finishes the second Huen Sao motion in the same way as before with a Fook Sao into the centre.

256. A third turning Huen Sao begins.

257. And is again is again finished with a Fook Sao motion back into the centre line.

258. The Left hand is placed on the Right arm.

259. The arm is cleared using two direction energy.

260. The Left palm is turned over.

261. The hand is folded back and begins to Huen Sao.

標指

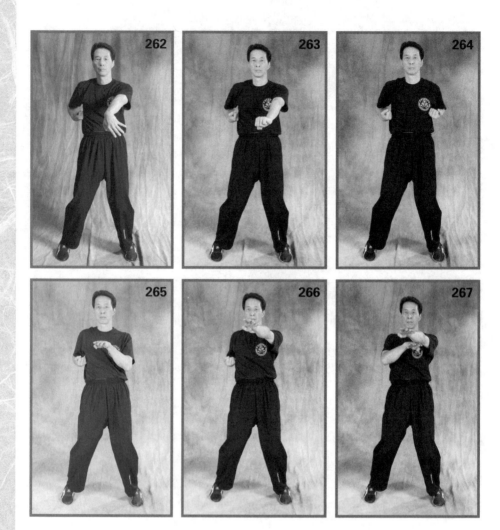

262. The Huen Sao circles round through the inside.

263. The hand is closed into a fist.

264. The hand is pulled back like a backwards elbow strike.

265. The left hand moves to the centre palm down.

266. The left hand shoots forward using last moment energy to finish the Biu Gee technique. Th fingers must be straight with the thumb tucked in.

267. The right hand moves palm down under the left elbow.

268. The right hand shoots forward as a Biu Sao (Biu Gee) while the left hand pulls back to under the right elbow.

269. The left hand now shoots forward as the right hand is pulled back to end next to the body. The speed at which the Biu Sao's are launched should be one ………two, three. i.e. one pause then two and three in quick succession.

270 - 271. The body turns to the right and delivers a neck height palm strike using the inside edge of the hand.

272. The hand then drops low.

273. A high Fak Sao is delivered to the left side from low on the right, cutting smoothly in front of the body and being led by the elbow. The hand is tipped slightly down and inwards as last moment energy is put into the Fak Sao (sometimes referred to as Mann Sao) motion.

標指

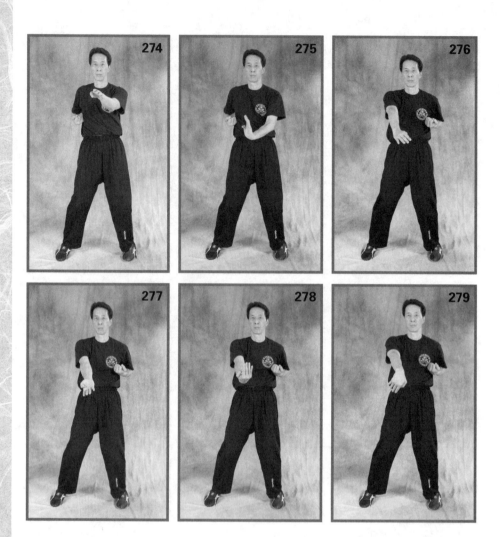

葉問詠春

274. The left hand Fook Sao returns to the centreline lead by the base of the thumb.

275. Once in the centreline the hand drops immediately into a sharp and short Jut Sao motion. This technique uses the base of the wrist with the fingers pointing up and the thumb tucked in.

276. The right hand is placed on the left arm palm up. The left arm is pulled back as the right hand shoots forward and turns over top face palm down.

277. The hand is turned over to face palm up.

278. The hand is folded back and a Huen Sao begins.

279. The Huen Sao circles through the inside.

280. The hand is closed into a fist.

281. The arm is withdrawn as an elbow strike.

282. The Right hand moves to the centre palm down. The Right hand then shoots forward using last moment energy to finish the Biu Gee technique. The fingers must be straight with the thumb tucked in.

283. The Left hand moves palm down under the Right elbow.

284. The Left hand shoots forward as a Biu Sao (Biu Gee) while the Right hand pulls back to under the Left elbow.

285. The Right hand now shoots forward as the Left hand is pulled back to end next to the body. The speed at which the Biu Sao's are launched should be one ....two, three. i.e. one pause then two and three in quick succession.

標指

286–287. The body turns to the Left and delivers a neck height palm strike using the inside edge of the hand.

288. The hand then drops low.

289. A high Fak Sao is delivered to the Right side from low on the Left, cutting smoothly in front of the body and being led by the elbow. The hand is tipped slightly down and inwards as last moment energy is put into the Fak Sao (sometimes referred to as Mann Sao) motion.

290. The Right hand Fook Sao returns to the centreline lead by the base of the thumb.

291. Once in the centreline the hand drops immediately into a sharp and short

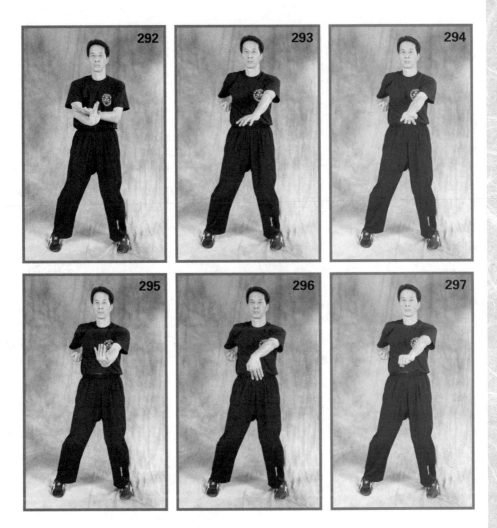

Jut Sao motion. This technique uses the base of the wrist with the fingers pointing up and the thumb tucked in.

292- 293. The Left hand is placed on the Right arm palm up. The Right arm is pulled back as the Left hand shoots forward and turns over top face palm down.

294. The hand is turned over to face palm up.

295. The hand is folded back and a Huen Sao begins.

296. The Huen Sao circles through the inside.

297. The hand is closed into a fist.

標指

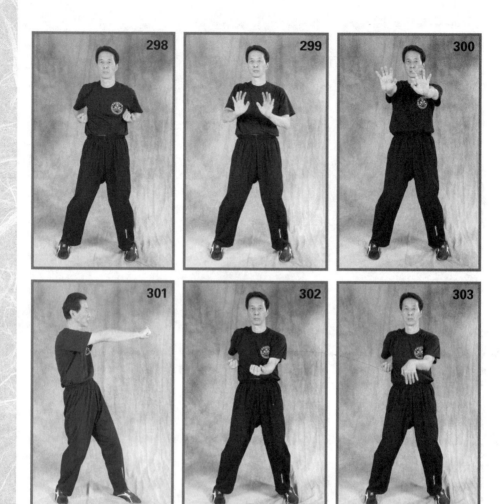

298. The arm is withdrawn as an elbow strike.

299. Both hands open and move in front of the body.

300. Both hands shoot forward and close as a grab.

301. Both hand then Lap Sao directly across (Ip Man style) the hands stay at shoulder height for this double Lap Sao. (Note: Some lineages double Lap Sao down to waist height then turning punch high).

302. The left hand then forms a fist and performs an arcing half circle punch back into the centre whilst the right hand is pulled back to the side of the body.

303. The hand is opened and folded down as the Huen Sao begins.

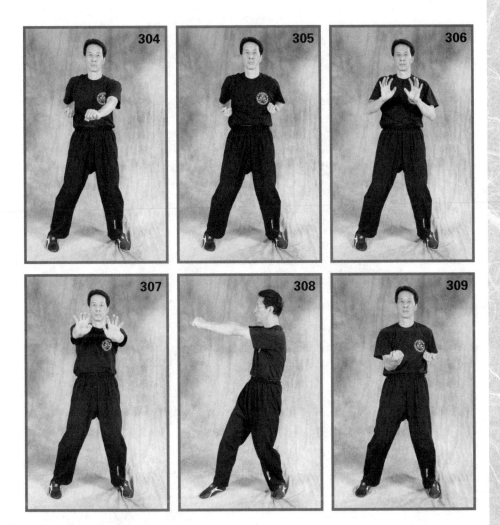

304. The Huen Sao is completed and the hand is closed into a fist.

305. The hand is withdrawn as a backwards elbow strike.

306. Both hands open and move in front of the body.

307. Both hands shoot forward and close as a grab.

308. Both hand then Lap Sao directly across (Ip Man style) the hands stay at shoulder height for this double Lap Sao. (Note: Some lineages double Lap Sao down to waist height then turning punch high).

309. The Right hand then forms a fist and performs an arcing half circle punch back into the centre whilst the Left hand is pulled back to the side of the body.

標指

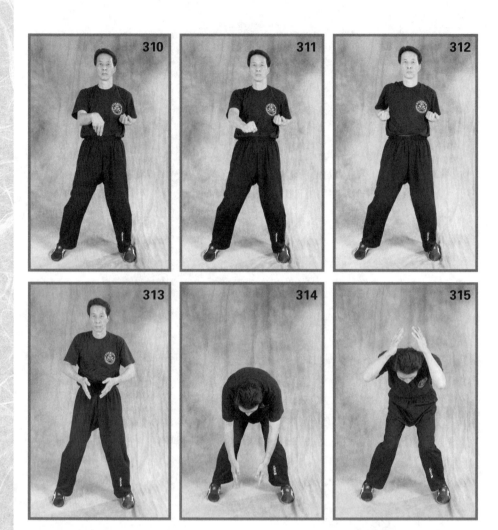

310. The hand is opened and folded down as the Huen Sao begins.

311. The Huen Sao is completed and the hand is closed into a fist.

312. The hand is withdrawn as a backwards elbow strike.

313. The hands begin to drop.

314. The body sinks to simulate a fall.

315. The body begins to stand up straight again and as it does the hands shoot upwards in conjunction with the head covering it from potential attack.

316. The head is covered by the arms all the way up to the position it started at which point the arms move outwards away from the head once the upward motion is completed.

317. The hand begin to drop for a second time.

318. The hands are in the downward position between the legs.

319. The hands rise with the head for a second time.

320. The motion is completed.

321. The hands begin to drop for the third time.

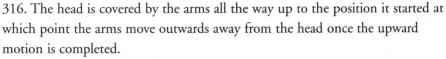

322. The body is low.

323. The hands rise with the head for a third time.

324. The third recover is completed.

325. The hands are circled round into the guard position in front of the body with the left hand forward.

326. A right punch is delivered down the centreline.

327. Left punch.

328. Right punch.

329. Left punch.

330. Finish chain punching with a right punch.

331. Open hand palm up.

332. Huen Sao begins .

333. The Huen Sao circles through the inside.

標指

334. The hand is closed into a fist.

335. The hand is pulled back as an elbow strike.

336. The stance is closed.

337. The arms are dropped and the body relaxes completely having completed the form.

BIU GEE APPLICATIONS

標指

1. Master Kwok blocks the opponents right jab with his Biu Sao

2–3. Using Yiu Ma (waist energy) Master Kwok performs a Lap Sao and simultaneous elbow attack

4–5 Shifting back Master Kwok pulls the opponents head to the rear and performs a simultaneous throat strike.

1. Master Kwok faces the opponent
2. The opponents punch is defended with a Fook Sao followed by a Jut Sao
3. The Jut Sao hand is thrust forward to strike the eyes as the Wu Sao (guarding hand) covers the opponents punching hand.

1. Master Kwok faces the opponent
2. The opponent delivers a right jab, which Master Kwok covers with the inside Jus Sao.
3. As the opponent launches a powerful cross punch, Master Kwok covers with Biu Sao and a simultaneous punch.

標指

A view from the opposite side of the technique demonstrated on page 227. Note how Master Kwok uses his Biu Ma (thrusting step) to add devastating power to the strike in photo 3.

1. Master Kwok and the opponent are in contact with both hands.

2–4. Master Kwok uses the Kop Jarn elbow movement from Biu Gee to trap the opponents hands and launch a strike.

標指

1. Master Kwok and the opponent face off.

2–3. The opponent attempts to grab the arm and secure an elbow lock.

4. Master Kwok quickly uses the left Biu Sao to free himself from the opponents grip.

5. Followed by a Lap Sao and Kop Jarn downward elbow strike.

1. Master Kwok faces the opponent.

2. As the opponent launches a straight punch, master Kwok sidesteps to create a superior angle for his counterattack.

3–4. Master Kwok steps in with Biu Ma and delivers a powerful palm strike to the opponents ribs whilst covering the punching hand with Tan Sao.

標指

1. Master Kwok's punch is blocked by the opponent.

2–3. The opponent grabs Master Kwok's arm and attempts to launch a strike to the head.

4–7. Master Kwok intercepts the punch with a Fak Sao / Pak Sao combined with the Biu Ma (thrusting step). This uproots the opponents balance and leaves him vulnerable to Master Kwok's counter attack, which could come in the form of a follow-up kick. This is an application of Biu Gee techniques, but is directly from the Wooden Dummy form.

標指

1. Master Kwok faces the opponent.

2. As the opponent launches a right punch, Master Kwok covers with a High / Low Gaun Sao.

3. Upon contact with the opponents arm, Master Kwok traps the hand and with an inside Lap Sao, steps in delivering a punch to the opponents head.

1. Master Kwok is attacked from the side by the opponent.

2. Master Kwok uses the turning Fak Sao movement from Biu Gee as a defensive maneuver.

3. Once contact is made with the opponents punching hand, Master Kwok uses Yiu Ma shifting energy to attack with a Lap Sao / Punch.

標指

1. Master Kwok faces off with the opponent.

2. As the opponent launches a punch, Master Kwok intercepts the arm using the double grab movement from Biu Gee.

3. Using Yiu Ma and double arm control, Master Kwok jerks the opponent off balance.

4. Once off balance the opponent is struck in the ribs with a powerful punch powered by Master Kwok's step, once again powered by his Yiu Ma.

1–3. Master Kwok demonstrates the use of a kick to finish the opponent after the "head clearing" movement from Biu Gee.

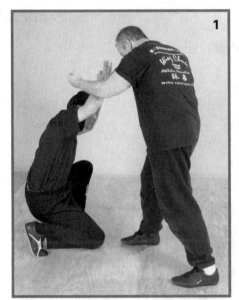

1–2. The opponent grabs Master Kwok and sweeps his front foot.

3. Catching himself, Master Kwok sees the opponent launching a punch to his head.

4–5. Master Kwok uses the "head clearing" movement from Biu Gee to regain his footing and control the opponent.

6. Finishing the opponent with a Lap Sao and punch.

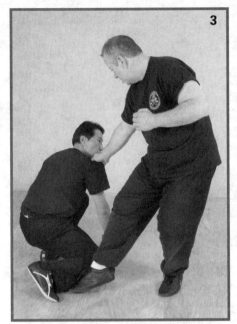

標指

CHAPTER 8

Mok Yan Jong—Testing the weapon

The 116 techniques that comprise the dummy form, as taught by the late Grandmaster Ip Man, make up an important part of the Wing Chun learning curve. The "dummy form" is often said to contain the fighting techniques of the Wing Chun system. This does not mean to say that the techniques learned in the three empty hand forms are not for fighting or combat, the difference is application. The empty hand forms have to be applied to a situation and cannot always be performed exactly as they appear in the form, whereas the techniques in the dummy form are performed against the 'Jong' or dummy, and are therefore being practiced in a way that applies them directly. This is a way of testing the skills learned in the empty hand forms. The dummy form is a way of giving impact or collision training to what is learned in the forms. This is because the techniques are performed against the physical arms, legs, and body of the wooden dummy. Therefore, the practitioner learns how to deal with impact and collision against a solid object such as an opponent.

The wooden dummy itself represents a physical opponent; its arms can represent attacks that have to be blocked, or obstacles for the practitioner to overcome in order to attack the trunk of the dummy. The leg of the dummy has to be maneuvered around and attacked by the practitioner during the form.

The advantages of training on a wooden dummy are:

It can be hit as hard as the practitioner wishes.

It can be trained on for long hours, whereas a live partner might get bored.

Because the dummy does not move much, the practitioner learns mobility while circling around the dummy in conjunction with blocking and striking hand techniques.

The dummy form contains applications from the three hand forms, along with some additional techniques like the neck pull and some additional kicks. Because of the angle and structure of the dummy, the trainee is naturally drawn to execute their techniques with correct positioning. Furthermore, because the dummy is a solid object, any mistakes in the practitioner's technique like incorrect angle, position of a block, or the wrong use of energy, are easily identifiable as it will result in a loss of balance or a clash of force causing pain. One mistake in the positioning of a block in the dummy form will often lead to the next move being harder to perform. Eventually, positioning and use of energy becomes perfect from training on the dummy. A live partner on the other hand, may not be able to identify mistakes if they are not experienced.

Grandmaster Samuel Kwok training on the Wooden Dummy.

Mook Yan Jong (Wooden Man Dummy)

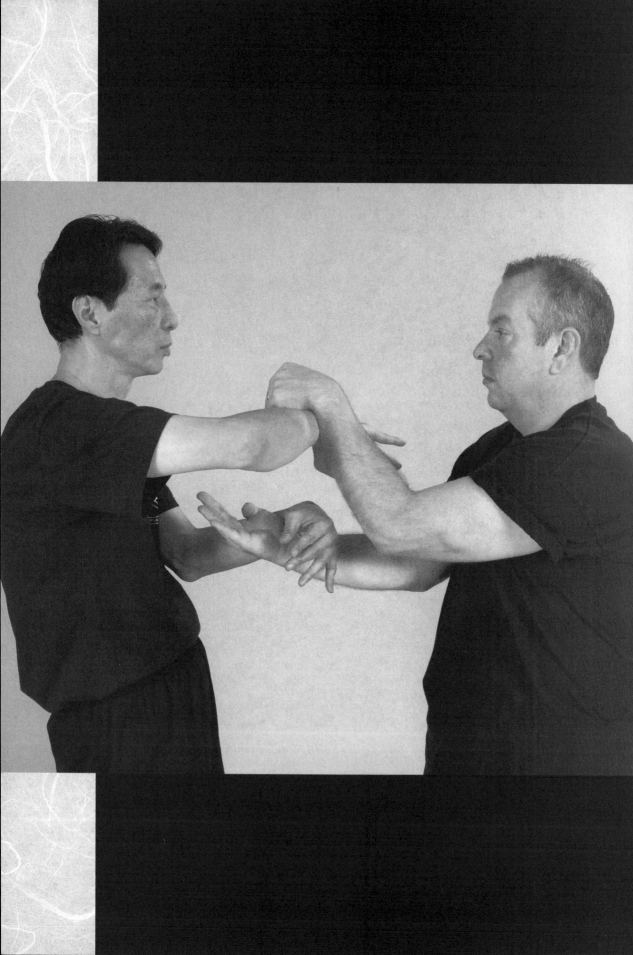

CHAPTER 9

Chi Sao—The Bridge Between Forms and Fighting

Chi Sao is one of the elements that set Wing Chun apart from other martial arts. It is a sensitivity exercise that develops conditioned reflex in a very short period of time. Chi Sao is the genius of the Wing Chun system.

Training in the three empty hand forms prepare the practitioner for Chi Sao, which in turn prepares them for fighting. Chi Sao is considered by many to be the most important aspect of training in the Wing Chun Kung Fu system. The training of the empty hand forms gives the student the tools needed to begin Chi Sao training. Through Chi Sao you learn the importance of being able to perform the 'turning' movement properly. In Chi Sao you have a training partner to help you refine your sensitivity and movements in order to increase your skill level. Chi Sao training is very similar to the application of Wing Chun in fighting, therefore it is important to include 'Chi Sao' as a regular part of training. It is also important to have your Instructor (Sifu) supervise your training and advise you why and how you have left 'openings' in your defense. Great Grandmaster Ip Man stated that, "the distance of fighting or sparring is the distance of Chi Sao." In fighting or sparring, reflex and sensitivity is the major advantage that enables the Wing Chun practitioner to defend themselves.

It was Grandmaster Ip Man's opinion that Chi Sao was the most important element of Wing Chun. He stated that, "Chi Sao was its intelligence, its genius." Therefore, this became a major focus in a student's learning process, and it would encompass a very large percentage of the program. Chi Sao training teaches the practitioner to react without thinking by way of the sensitivity developed during training. The practitioner learns to redirect the energy that is oncoming, and direct that energy into their own counter attack. In Chi Sao, the student learns to utilize the Faan Sao (Returning Hand) technique in conjunction with the footwork, and Yiu Ma (Waist Energy) developed by proper stance turning. Chi Sao is a special training method unique to Wing Chun. It is often confused with the "pushing hand" techniques of Tai Chi, but the two are very different.

The term "sticking hands" is often used to describe the Chi Sao exercise. It must be made clear that Chi Sao is not in itself a method of fighting; it is a method of training to develop sensitivity of the arms so that you can feel your opponent's intentions and sense the proper response without mental deliberation. Chi Sao teaches correct elbow structure and position. Mastery of elbow control and positioning is Chi Sao's secret ingredient. The Chi Sao 'exercise' teaches the use of the proper type of energy, and helps the student recognize weaknesses in the opponent's structure. Chi Sao also teaches the student the concept of defending with the minimum motion or effort.

Grandmaster Ip Chun emphasizes, "It is important not to mistake the goal of Chi Sao. Too many people use their Chi Sao as a competition and concentrate on trying to score points by hitting their training partner. In a juvenile way, they feel the need to prove themselves. This defeats the chief goal of Chi Sao training, the development of feeling and sensitivity." Quite often contact made is far too heavy and the practitioners become head hunters, trying to hit each other in the face. This can lead to injuries because of the lack of control that is inherent in this type of practise. This type of training prevents the individual from attaining a relaxed, confident, and realistic approach to fighting. An aggressive attitude of this kind is not compatible with the philosophy of the Ip Man Family Wing Chun Kung Fu style, and it dramatically impedes the learning process and progress of the individual.

It is important to remember that there are no fixed patterns of movements in Chi Sao, and this relates closely to real fighting. It is essential to remember that Chi Sao should always be practiced with control and maintained as a separate concept, distinct from sparring or free-fighting, where the aim in the latter case is to hit your opponent. In Chi Sao the aim is to control your opponent! Grandmaster Ip Ching states, "Just because you can hit the opponent, it doesn't mean you can control him, but if you can control him, you can hit him anytime you want." This is why Ip Man called Chi Sao the skill of Wing Chun, Chi Sao teaches how to gain control of the opponent.

The three forms give us the necessary tools for Chi Sao training, which in turn prepares us for application of Wing Chun in a fight. Wing Chun does not incorporate any 'fancy or flowery' techniques, and Chi Sao is unparalleled for training for sensitivity, which is needed to apply Wing Chun in a violent encounter.

Gradual and systematic training of Chi Sao helps the practitioner develop the necessary skills that allow them to become a complete Wing Chun fighter. In the early stages, simple concepts and principles such as correct positions, becoming sensitive to the partner's energy, and proper use of their own energy are taught. The basic techniques are introduced once the simple rolling movements and reflexes start to become second nature. Progress in Chi Sao will depend upon the practitioner developing reflexes and responses 'sensitivity' that relate to the dynamic interaction with their training partner. Bruce Lee described Chi Sao in the following way, "When the opponent expands, I contract. When he contracts, I expand." It is not a wrestling match, but a blending with the opponent in order to dissolve their attack and use the "path of least resistance" in applying our counter attack. Again, what Bruce Lee described as "the art of fighting without fighting!"

According to Grandmaster Ip Ching, "The purpose of Chi Sao is to apply the techniques of the three empty hand forms and the turning movements of Chum Kiu. In addition, it teaches you four things:

Correct way of using energy.

To develop good sensitivity (i.e. not using strength against strength—to use the other person's energy against them)

To develop good positioning of both the hands and the feet.

To develop good hand techniques that can be applied in any situation.

Chi Sao, if done properly, teaches you how to react automatically. Chi Sao is the practical application of the techniques learned in the forms. Chi Sao teaches the Wing Chun practitioner to use their techniques in a way that is not static or pre-arranged, but alive and dynamic. Chi Sao should be used as an opportunity to enhance your skills—it is not in itself fighting, but rather a way of training your techniques in a way which will improve your ability to apply Wing Chun in a fight. Chi Sao ultimately trains for unconscious competence. An idea we looked at in the chapter about the learning process.

Dan Chi Sao (Single Sticking Hand)

1. Master Kwok is in the Tan Sao position, balancing Sifu Massengill's Fook Sao.

2. Master Kwok launches a palm strike towards the chest. Sifu Massengill dissolves the energy with Jut Sao.

3. Sifu Massengill launches a punch towards Master Kwok's chest, which Master Kwok dissolves with his Bong Sao.

4. Both return to the original starting position of Tan Sao / Fook Sao.

5. A close up of the Tan Sao and Fook Sao positions.

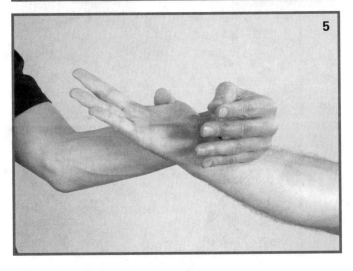

Seung Chi Sao (Double Hand Sticking Hands)
One hand inside, one hand outside cycle

1. Master Kwok—Left High Fook Sao / Right Tan Sao

Sifu Massengill—Left Fook Sao / Right Bong Sao

2. Master Kwok—Left Low Fook Sao / Right Bong Sao

Sifu Massengill—Left High Fook Sao / Right Tan Sao

3. Return to positions in photo #1.

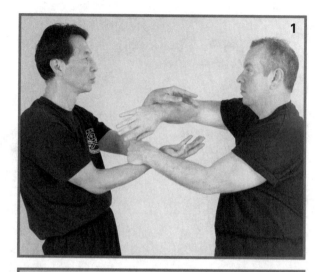

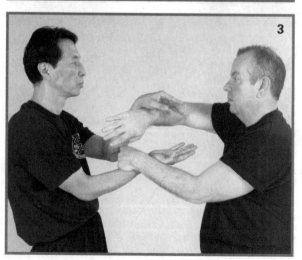

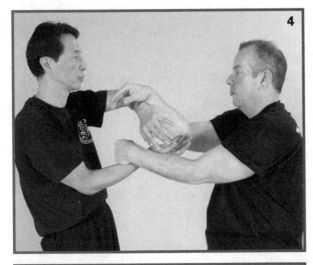

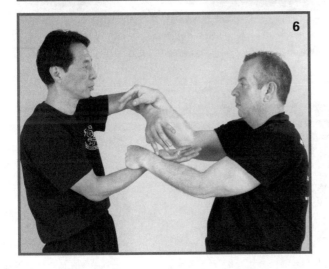

Both hands inside / Both hands outside

1. Master Kwok—Inside Left Bong Sao / Right Tan Sao

Sifu Massengill—Outside Left Low Fook Sao / Right High Fook Sao

2. Master Kwok—Inside Left Tan Sao / Right Bong Sao

Sifu Massengill—Outside Left High Fook Sao / Right Low Fook Sao

3. Return to positions in photo #1

Lop Sao Drill

1. Master Kwok—Left Punch

Sifu Massengill—Right Bong Sao / Left Wu Sao

2. Sifu Massengill shoots the Wu Sao hand forward to contact Master Kwok's punching hand.

3. Sifu Massengill performs a simultaneous Left Lop Sao / Right Straight Punch

Master Kwok dissolves Sifu Massengill's punch with his Left Bong Sao and brings his Right hand back to a Wu Sao guard.

4. Master Kwok shoots the Wu Sao hand forward to contact Sifu Massengill's punching hand.

5. Master Kwok performs a simultaneous Right Lop Sao / Left Straight Punch

Sifu Massengill dissolves Master Kwok's punch with his Right Bong Sao and brings his Left hand back to a Wu Sao guard. (Which returns them to the starting position from photo #1)

CHAPTER 10

Fann Sao

Earlier the term Faan Sao (or returning hand) was mentioned. Fann Sao is an important concept for a Wing Chun practitioner, and is used in Chi Sao and sparring. In fact it is essential in higher levels of Chi Sao. Which of course means it is an important aspect of fighting in a real situation. But what is meant by the term Faan Sao?

For a basic definition, Faan Sao describes follow up techniques or "the continued controlling and attacking of an opponent." Continuation is the essence of Faan Sao. For example, after performing a Bong Sao to Lap Sao and Fak Sao strike in Chi Sao or real fight situation, a few options will present themselves. One thing that may happen is the opponent blocks, or they may be unable to avoid the Fak Sao strike and get hit by it. From this point there are more options. The first option is to do nothing; the second option is to break contact, perhaps to attack again. However, as a Wing Chun practitioner this is a bad move as Wing Chun specializes in close contact combat. Furthermore, it could lead to getting hit by a counter attack. The better option is to perform Faan Sao or follow up techniques, i.e. if a block is felt, the energy of the Fak Sao should be stopped and immediately relaxed, and then changed into a different technique such as a Lap Sao and palm strike with the other hand. If this is blocked, one could perhaps Lap and Fak, but the point is not what particular technique is

performed. Instead, if an obstruction like a block appears, one should not try to force the attack through, instead use Faan Sao and follow up with something else. Therefore, when performing Faan Sao you are training a reflex response. At first the practitioner has to think about what to do when contact is achieved. This is the conscious competence level that was described earlier. Eventually the practitioner will simply respond without thinking, 'he has blocked so I will lap and strike'; this becomes a reflex after enough training—this reflex is the essence of Faan Sao. At this point unconscious competence is achieved. The idea is that in a fight one will just react and deal with the situation instead of having to stop and think or analyze the situation as this takes time. In a real fight it is the fraction of a second that makes the difference between getting hit or not, and to hitting or not hitting.

When training Faan Sao remember that even if the attack is successful due to Faan Sao, do not stop the attack if the opponent still represents a threat. Also, don't break away to strike again, instead use Faan Sao to control the opponent's hand, and strike for example with a Gum Sao and palm strike, then swap over so that the striking hand returns as a Gum Sao, and the previous pinning hand strikes, and so on until the desired result is achieved.

Faan Sao techniques are to some extent found in the dummy form, for example the arm of the dummy is lapped and a throat chop is delivered with the other hand, then the chopping hand returns to the same arm controlling it with a Pak Sao as the previously lapping hand performs a spade hand strike.

Using Fan Sao follow up techniques is essential in Chi Sao and fighting for controlling your opponent. It is also used for breaking through any obstacles like hands, for example an opponent's guard or blocks that may get in the way.

Ip Man believed one of the most important aims of Chi Sao was to train the speed and technique and eventual unconscious reflex of Faan Sao. So remember:

"If your Faan Sao is fast you can use it in a fight,
but if your technique is bad, it will just be a mess."

The Difference Between Strength and Ging

Strength is represented by a person's muscles, for example the triceps in the arms, the deltoids in the shoulders, and lateral muscles of the back. Ging however, represents the transfer of energy from the legs using the strength of the body to put power and energy into the strikes, kicks and blocks.

Therefore, it is not how much strength you have that defines how good at martial arts you are, it is how much Ging you have.

Ging is not continuous or permanent, and when you use it unlike muscles, there is no fatigue. Once you have it you have it for life. We need only look at footage of the late grandmaster Ip Man just weeks before he died. The power he hit the wooden dummy with was phenomenal, especially for a person so close to death. This is because Ip Man had good Ging as he was a great martial artist.

In martial arts it is all about Ging, strength alone is not good enough for fighting. You do not need big muscles; you just need to use what you have effectively. Therefore, you do not need to do lots of weight training; you just need to develop good Ging. Dim Mak strikes use Ging to deliver accurate power for internal damage. The strikes must be as fast as an arrow.

Strength is from the back, and you drive it to the fingers through the application of Ging. This is the hard part. Wing Chun's third form Biu Gee develops Ging.

The character above represents strength, and the penetrating arrow like symbol on the left shows how to use the strength. Together the symbol represents Ging.

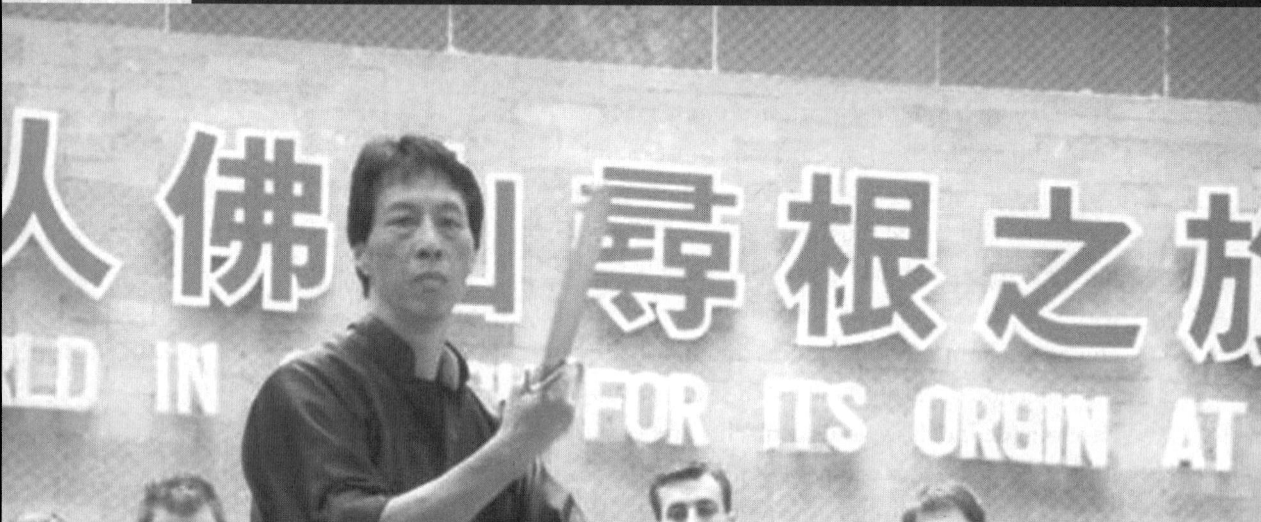
尋根之
FOR ITS

CHAPTER 11

A Demonstration to Help the Promotion of the Ip Man Tong

If you were a Wing Chun practitioner and I said the words, "what is Fat Shan (Foshan) famous for", you would probable say, "Ip Man or Wing Chun." But to the local people of Fat Shan City in China, it is just as famous for its pottery, clothing and metal industry as it is for its martial arts heritage.

Many famous martial artists of Southern China are from Fat Shan, including, naming but a few: Wong Fei Hung of the Hung Kuen style, Tam Sham of the Choy Lay Fat style, Leung Jan, Chan Wah Shan, and Ip Man of the Wing Chun style.

On the 3rd of November 2001, students and instructors of the Samuel Kwok Martial Art Association arrived in Hong Kong. The group was not just from England, but also from the United States, Switzerland, and Germany. The whole trip was organized and lead by Sifu Samuel Kwok and Sifu Ip Ching.

The purpose of this trip was to visit the Wing Chun community and help in the promotion of the Ip Man Tong (Ip Man Museum) in Fat Shan, as well as to train with Sifu Ip Ching at the famous Ching Woo School, which is about 80 years old and who's founder was Fok Yuen Gap.

The Ching Woo School is a place where many different styles of martial arts

葉問詠春

have trained; also many masters from northern and southern China have trained and taught at this great school. Sifu Ip Ching taught and practiced Siu Lim Tao, Chum Kiu, Biu Gee, and Chi Sau techniques. It was a great honour for us to be able to train at the Ching Woo School, and with the local Wing Chun community coming along to share the experience, it was a very memorable two days.

We were then asked to demonstrate Sifu Ip Man's Wing Chun for the Fat Shan's local community at the famous Ancestral Temple, which is over 900 years old and full of history. The whole event was organized by the Fat Shan Ancestral Museum Committee, headed by Chairman Leung. The Wong Fei Hung Museum of Martial Arts, headed by Lo Kueng, came to greet us with a traditional lion dance and took part in the demonstrations. Sifu Garry McKenzie from London England, who also brought several students with him, helped with the interpretation on the microphone, due to the fact that he can speak fluent Cantonese.

On the day before the demonstration, Sifu Ip Ching and Sifu Samuel Kwok had a meeting with Chairman Leung, to discuss the matter of the Ip Man Tong.

葉問詠春 Grandmaster Samuel Kwok Traditional Ip Man Wing Chun Association www.ipmanwingchun.com

At first the committee said, "It would be at least 18 months before they could decide on a date, due to other projects they have to organize." Sifu Ip Ching then suggested they could organize a temporary site for the Ip Man Tong until they had decided on a permanent site; they said, "They would take the matter under consideration."

After the day of the demonstration, which consisted of a whole range of Wing Chun techniques, and seeing the huge amount of public support and interest, as well as being televised, the chairman of the Fat Shan Ancestral Museum Committee had a second meeting with Sifu Ip Ching and Sifu Samuel Kwok. He felt that Sifu Ip Man's Wing Chun, which has been taught all over the world, and that by Building the Ip Man Tong could affect the prosperity and tourism of Fat Shan.

In late November 2001, the Fat Shan Ancestral Museum Committee invited the Ip Man Tong Development Council to discuss a location inside the museum for the Building of the Ip Man Tong and an official opening date was given as 9th November 2002.

The Ip Man Tong Development Council would like to invite all Sifu Ip Man's lineage of Wing Chun from overseas, to come to Fat Shan and visit the Ip Man Tong inside the Ancestral Museum and take part in all the activities, to help in the promotion of the Ip Man Tong and Kung Fu in Fat Shan.

CHAPTER 12

Lineage—The True Test of Authenticity

"You must know the source of the water from which you drink"
—Ip Man

**Family Tree of the Samuel Kwok Martial Arts Association
And Traditional Ip Man Wing Chun Association**

Family Tree of the Samuel Kwok Lineage
Ip Man
Ip Chun & Ip Ching
Samuel Kwok

United Kingdom Students
Shabir Akhtar
Leo Au Yeung   Reading
Richard Baines   Sheffield
Stephen Bentley   Leeds

Dereck Bradley	Devon
Tony O'Brien	Blackpool
Martin Brieley	Leeds
Steven Colton	Colne
Danny Conner	
William Davidson	Manchester
Steven Dyde	Nuneaton/Coverntry
Andrew Edwards	Sheffield
Adam Gregor	Lancaster
Tom Hamilton	Scotland
Mark Hyland	Folkstone
Trevor Jefferson	Mallorca
Peter Jones	Rugby
Dan Knight	Lancaster
Ronold Kho	London
Carlos Lewis	Sheffield
Martin Lloyd	Worcester
Steven Lyons	Bournemouth
Dereck O' Hanlon	Manchester
Steven Rigby	Preston
Paul Smith	Scotland
Sandy Teenan	Scotland
Anthony Warwick	Coventry
Wan Li	Manchester
Peter Wade	Great Yarmouth
Steve Williams	Liverpool

Overseas

Juan Jose Bonet Vidal	Spain
Bang Chiu	Vietnam
Guy Diddot	Johannesburg, South Africa
Chris Damiano	Florida, USA
Horst Dresher	Germany
Ole Dupoint	Denmark
Apad Feher	Hungry
Rick Frye	Arizona, USA
Josef Flecken	Germany

David Gallaher	Florida, USA
Martin Gilmore	Perth, Australia
Matt Johnson	Chicago,USA
Tony Massengill	Virginia, USA
Mike Davies	Florida, USA
Armen Minasjan	Germany
Philip Nearing	Chicago, USA
Mikkel Nielson	Denmark
Ole Dupoint	Denmark
Joe Oliver	Caribbean
Lex Reinhart	France/Switzerland
Antonio Sardos	Portugal
Yeung Wai Kwun	Hong Kong

CHAPTER 13

Samuel Kwok's Photo Album

Thanks to Grandmasters Ip Chun and Ip Ching for many of the photos presented here.

Young Ip Man.

The only photo of Ip Man in Western Clothes.

Grandmaster Ip Man in his later years.

Grandmaster Ip Man with his most personal students, his sons Ip Chun and Ip Ching.

Ip Man in formal Portrait.

Ip Man with his most famous student, Bruce Lee.

Bruce Lee paying his respects to Ip Man on a trip to Hong Kong.

Photos taken from the 8MM film made for his sons just 10 days prior to his death.

葉問詠春

Young Ip Chun.

*Ip Chun on his first visit to Europe here
with his top student Samuel Kwok.*

Photos of Ip Chun at the Hong Kong Athletic Association.

*Ip Chun demonstrating the
Wing Chun Knife form as
Samuel Kwok looks on.*

*Ip Chun, Samuel Kwok and
Group on roof in Hong Kong.*

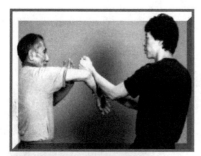

Ip Chun and Samuel Kwok training.

Founder fellows of the Society of Martial Arts at Salford University.

Ip Chun with Samuel Kwok at Hong Kong Athletic Association.

葉問詠春

Ip Chun and Samuel Kwok demonstrate at the Ip Man Tong in Foshan, China.

*Ip Man with Ip Ching
early 1960's.*

Ip Man with Ip Ching and family.

Ip Ching with Samuel kwok during a training session early 1990s.

Ip Ching with Samuel Kwok at U.S. Seminar. (Note: Samuel Kwok was the first to bring Ip Chun and Ip Ching to Europe and the U.S.)

Ip Ching working privately with
Senior Student Samuel Kwok.

Samuel Kwok training the Wing Chun knives
with Ip Ching. (Note: The knives pictured
were a gift to Samuel from Ip Ching.
They were a pair of knives which belonged
to his father, Grandmaster Ip Man.)

Ip Ching and Samuel Kwok training Chi Sao.

Ip Ching performing
a joint lock.

Ip Ching with Samuel
Kwok at Ip Ching's
home in Hong Kong.

Ip Ching teaching the
Biu Gee form.

Ip Ching with Samuel Kwok at the Ip Man Tong in Foshan, China.

At Ip Man's Grave.

Hong Kong seminar 2005.

With his two teachers Grandmasters Ip Chun and Ip Ching.

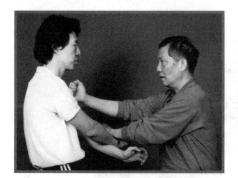

With Ip Ching and Tsui Sheung Tien.

Training with Ip Ching.

Young Samuel Kwok.

Samuel Kwok demonstrating Biu Gee.

With Wong Shun Leung.

With Moy Yat in New York.

With Kung Fu film star Sammo Hung.

Samuel Kwok with disciple Tony Massengill and Jet Li's teacher Wu Bin.

*Samuel Kwok demonstrating at the opening
of the Ip Man Tong in Foshan, China.*

Celebrating the opening of the Ip Man Tong with his teacher, Ip Ching.

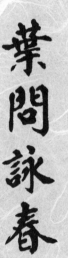

Demonstrating at the World Wing Chun Conference,
Hong Kong 2005.

*Samuel Kwok and students visit the Ylu Kay Wing chun school
in Foshan, China for a Technical Exchange.*

*Samuel Kwok with friend,
the late Carlson Gracie
at Double Impact Seminar
they conducted together.*

*Samuel Kwok with Carlson Gracie
in Kwok Association shirt.*

"Carlson Loves Wing Chun,"
written by Carlson Gracie on the
back of Samuel Kwok's car.

With Carlson Gracie in front
of Big Ben in London.

Double Impact Seminar Group Photo.

Samuel Kwok with European disciple Billy Davidson.

Samuel Kwok with American disciple
Tony Massengill.

Morning Walk with his teacher Ip Ching, in Hong Kong park.

CHAPTER 14

A Chronicle of the Life of Ip Man

Written by Ip Chun / Translated by Samuel Kwok
Born October 1893, died December 1972, Aged 79 years.

Grandmaster Ip Man spent his whole life as champion of the cause of Wing Chun Kung Fu. He was responsible for advancing Wing Chun Kung Fu to its' eminence today. Throughout the world, students of Wing Chun Kung Fu continue to publish articles about Grandmaster Ip Man, his life and achievements. Therefore to celebrate the 100th anniversary of the birth of Grandmaster Ip Man this chronicle is being produced for all those interested in Wing Chun Kung Fu.

This chronicle is about Ip Man and his contribution to the style of Wing Chun Kung Fu. Therefore the details of his life, his education and profession, will be only be covered in brief. There are thousands of practitioners of Wing Chun Kung Fu and those who are not mentioned in this tribute must bear with the author for lack of space.

He was born on October 14th 1893 in the Ching Dynasty (Kand Shoui—September 5th in the Chinese calendar) in Fut Shan town in Kwong Tung province which was then in Lam Hoi county. So Ip Man's birthplace is often referred to as Lam Hoi in Kwong Tung.

Grandmaster Ip Man's father was called Ip Oi Dor, his mother was Ng Shui, he was one of four brothers and sisters. His brother was called Gei Gak (Grandmaster Ip Man was originally called Gei Man). His sister's name was Wan Mei (Sik Chung)

• 1899 to 1905 (Ching Kwong Shui)
Grandmaster Ip Man 6 to 12 years old.
Location: Fut Shan.
Grandmaster Ip Man studied Wing Chun Kung Fu with Chan Wah Shun
(Money Changer Wan). The location was in Fut Shan town main street
(song Yun Dai Gai) in the Ip family hall. The garden in now owned by the government and the hall is no longer there. At the time studying together with Grandmaster Ip Man were Lui Yui Chai, Ng Chung Sao, Ng Siu Lo and others.

• 1905 (Ching Kwon Shui)
Grandmaster Ip Man at 12 years old.
Location: Fut Shan.
Chan Wah Shun passed away, but before he died he asked Ng Chung Sao to helpIp Man to complete the Wing Chun system. Chan Wah Shun's body was taken by his Kung Fu disciples to Chan village in Shun Dak, for burial.

• 1937 (Man Kwok year 26)
Grandmaster Ip Man 44 years old.
Location: Fut Shan.
The Japanese invaded south China.

• 1937 to 1945 (Man Kwok year 26 to 34)
Grandmaster Ip Man 44 to 52 years old.
Location: Fut Shan.
For 8 years Ip Man fought the Japanese but Fut Shan was occupied and ruled by a puppet government. The Grandmaster swore not to be used by the puppet government so he became very poor and often he went hungry. Luckily his good friend, Chow Cheng Chung, gave him food from time to time. Grandmaster Ip Man wanted to repay his kindness and so accepted his son, Chow Kwang Yiu, as his student. From 1941 to 1943 he taught Wing Chun Kung Fu in the cotton mill at Wing On. At this time studying with Chow

Kwong Yiu were Kwok Fu, Chan Chi Sun, Ng Ying, Lun Kai, Chow Sai and others. These were the firstgeneration of students that Grandmaster Ip Man taught. Kwok Fu and Lun Kai are still alive and teaching Wing Chun Kung Fu in China today, in Kwong Chow, Fut Shan.

- **1945 (Man Kwok year 34)**
Grandmaster Ip Man is 52 years old.
Location: Fut Shan.
The year Japan surrendered.

- **1945 to 1949 (Man Kwok year 34 to 38)**
Grandmaster Ip Man 52 to 56 years old.
Location: Kwong Chow, Fut Shan.
During this period of time, Grandmaster Ip Man was at his busiest at work, even though he loved Wing Chun Kung Fu he had to leave it for a time. Until, in 1948, through his very good friend Tong Kai, he was introduced to Pang Lam who begged Ip Man to teach him Wing Chun Kung Fu. Through this busy time, Ip Man coached Pang Lam on the form at the Fut Shang Cheung Yee Athletic Association.

- **1949 (Man Kwok year 38)**
Grandmaster Ip Man is 56 years old.
Location: Macao and Hong Kong.
Grandmaster Ip Man went through Macao to Hong Kong but while in Macao he stayed for two weeks at Cho Doi Street with friends who owned a bird shop.

- **1950 to 1953 (Man Kwok year 39 to 42)**
Grandmaster Ip Man 57 to 60 years old.
Location: Hong Kong.
In July 1950, through Lee Man's introduction, Grandmaster Ip Man started teaching in Dai Lam Street, Kowloon. The first Wing Chun Kung Fu class was for the Restaurant Workers Association. When he opened the class there were only 8 people including Leung Shang and Lok Yiu. All these were restaurant workers, but later he was joined by Tsui Shan Tin, Ip Bo Ching, Chiu Wan, Lee Yan Wing, Law Peng, Man Siu Hung and others. This period of time was called

the forefront of the Restaurant Workers Association. Grandmaster Ip Man also taught in the Restaurant Workers, Shang Wan branch, Union HQ in Hong Kong. Students included Lee Wing, Yue May Keng, Lee Leung Foon and others.

- **1953 to 1954 (Man Kwok year 42 to 43)**
Grandmaster Ip Man 60 to 61 years old.
Location: Hong Kong.
When Leung Sheung was defeated in the union elections, Grandmaster Ip Man moved the school to Hoi Tan Street. Learning at that time were Wong Shun Leung, Wong Kiu, Wong Chaok, Ng Chan and others. Ip Man also taught private lessons at Three Prince Temple on Yue Chow Street. Students were Lee Hong and others.

- **1954 to 1955 (Man Kwok year 43 to 44)**
Grandmaster Ip Man 61 to 62 years old.
Location: Hong Kong.
Leung Sheung was re-elected chairman of the Restaurant Workers union and so Grandmaster Ip Man moved back to the union HQ. This is called the later stage of the Restaurant Workers Association. At this time he was joined by Lee Kam Sing, Kan Wa Jeet (Victor Kan), Lo Man Kam, Cheung Cheuk Heng(William Cheung) and others.

- **1955 to 1957 (Man Kwok year 44 to 46)**
Grandmaster Ip Man 62 to 64 years old.
Location: Hong Kong.
Grandmaster Ip Man moved the school to Lee Tat Street, Yao Ma Tei in Kowloon.
The students here were Lee Siu Lung (Bruce Lee), Chan Shing, Haw Kin Cheung, Siu Yuk Man, Poon Bing Lid, Pang Kam Fat and others.

- **1957 to 1962 (Man Kwok year 46 to 51)**
Grandmaster Ip Man 64 to 69 years old.
Location: Hong Kong.
During this 5 years Ip Man moved the school to Lee Chang Oak Chuen. At this time students were Mek Po, Yeung Hei, Moi Yat, Ho Kam Ming and others. During this period of time Grandmaster Ip Man taught mostly private lessons.

Sau Kei Wan, Shun Kei pottery shop. Students were Wong Pak Yee, Wong Wei, Yeung Chung Han, Chow Lok Gee, Wong Kwok Yau and others.

Tsim ha Tsui, Bong Lak Hong. Students were Tong Cho Chi, Lee Fat Chi, Chang Tak Chiu, Tam Lai and others.

3 Tai Po Road. Students were Chung Kam Chuen, Chung Wing Hong.

- **1962 to 1963 (Man Kwok year 51 to 52)**
Grandmaster Ip Man 69 to 70 years old.
Location: Hong Kong.
Grandmaster Ip Man moved the school to 61 Tai Po Road, a unit in the Heng Ip building. Students were Cheung Yiu Wing, Ho Luen, Jun Ching On, Chan Woon Lam, Chang Tai Yim and Kwok See Yan. Private lessons were taught at Yee Wa tailor's shop at Tsim Sha Tsui. Students were Peter Chang and a group of people from Po Lak Hong.

- **1963 to 1965 (Man Kwok year 52 to 54)**
Grandmaster Ip Man 70 to 72 years old.
Location: Hong Kong.
The school was moved to the top floor of the Tai Sang restaurant on Fook Chuen Street, Tai Kok Tsui. Originally this had been the storeroom. The owner was called Ho Luen who let them use the room. Most of the people from the school at the Heng Ip building also moved here. As well as Ho Luen there were also Yeung Chung Hon, Wat Yung Sung, Pang Kam Fat, Jun Ching On, Lee Yan Wing and Yau Hak So. During this period of time Grandmaster Ip Man also taught students, mainly from the police, privately at San Po Kong, Hin Hing Street. These included Tang Sang, Lam Ying Fat, Yuen Chi Kong, Lee Yiu Fei, Wong Kok and others.

- **1965 to 1972 (Man Kwok year 54 to 61)**
Grandmaster Ip Man 72 to 79 years old.
Location: Hong Kong.
The school at the Tai Sang restaurant finished and Grandmaster Ip Man moved to live on Tung Choi Street residence because he was getting old. Although he was already partly retired he was still teaching one to one private tuition. Going to Ip Man's home during this period of time, were Wong Chung Wah (Yat Oak Goi Tse), Wong Hei,Hong Jap Sum and others. He also went out teaching to three places:

1. The Ving Tsun Athletic Association, which, in 1967, was the first martial arts society to be officially registered with the government. The Ving Tsun Athletic Association then decided to open Kung Fu classes at the association's address. The association placed Grandmaster Ip Man in charge of the instruction. Assisting him were Jun Ching On, Fung Hon, Wong Hon Chung and others. This was only about three months.

2. Chan Wei Hong's home on Waterloo Road, Learning here were Chen Wei Hong, the Siu Lung brothers, also Wong Chi On, Chan Kam Ming, Chung Yau, Lau Hon Lam,Man Yim Kwong and others.

Grandmaster Ip Man relaxing with Ip Ching in the suburbs of Hong Kong (Early 1960s).

3. Chi Yau Road. When Chan Wei Hong had other business and could not continue at Waterloo Road, Grandmaster Ip Man moved to the roof top of Lau Hon Lam'shome. Joining here were Wong Chi Ming and he also officially accepted a female student called Ng Yuet Dor.

4. Siu Fai Toi. At solicitor Ip Sing Cheuk's house. Apart from Ip Sing Cheuk the rest of the students were also mostly solicitors. This was the last place that Grandmaster Ip Man taught Wing Chun Kung Fu.

Grandmaster Ip Man passed away at his home on Tung Choi Street on the 1st December 1972 (Man Kwok year 61). 26th October in the Chinese lunar calendar. He enjoyed 79 years of life.

Grandmaster Samuel Kwok with Ip Man's original pair of knives. (A gift to Kwok from Grandmaster Ip Ching.)

Traditional Ip Man Wing Chun Association

詠 春

Ip Family / Samuel Kwok Lineage

CHAPTER 15

Glossary of Techniques in Chinese Alphabetical Order

Biu Sao

The Biu Sao or thrusting fingers is one of the many Wing Chun moves which can be used both as a block and as a strike. It can be used to strike or block anything around shoulder height or above. Or it can be used to strike to the eyes and throat.

Bong Sao

The Bong Sao or wing arm is quite a complex Wing Chun movement that features largely in the system's forms.

Fak Sao

The Fak Sao is a chop that first learnt from Sil Lim Tao Wing Chun's first form. A good move to use when the practitioner is unsure of what is coming, this move is similar but not the same as the Mann Sao.

Fook Sao

The fook Sao or bridge-on arm is relatively simple but effective Wing Chun movement that features largely in the system's first form. It is primarily used in chi Sao but can be applied as a block.

Gaun Sao (low)

The low Gaun Sao or Splitting block is used to block attacks to the mid section. It is an essential part of the Wing Chun blocking arsenal.

Gaun Sao (high)

The high Gaun Sao or Splitting block is slightly more complex block than its lower counterpart, hence it is found in the third form and not the first. But when both gaun Sao's are performed together they can cover and block almost any attack on the body.

Gum Sao

The gum Sao or pinning hand is found in the first form and is used as a block or to pin an opponents arm (hence its name), It is often used in chi Sao.

Huen Sao

The Huen Sao or circling hand is an essential Wing Chun technique found throughout the systems 3 hand forms. It can be performed clockwise or anti-clockwise depending on the situations need.

Ju-Cheung

Ju-Cheung is a powerful 'sideward palm' strike that uses the heel of the palm to strike an opponent.

Jum Sao

The Jum Sao is yet another technique which can be used both as a block and a strike however, it is one of the few Wing Chun blocks which is performed with power, that is not to say the block uses a clash of force just that power is applied to 'strike' when blocking to cause damage the aggressor.

Jut Sao

The Jut Sao or sinking hand is an extremely effective block which can throw the balance of the opponent whilst leaving the practitioners hand in the perfect place for a counter strike.

Kop Sao

The Cop Sao or downward hand is a movement found in the second form Chun Kiu. The Cop Sao is not strictly a technique in its own right it is a blend of Gum Sao, Pak Sao and Jut Sao. The cup Sao can be applied practically and it is also used in Chi Sao.

Kop Jarn

Kop Jarn is a downward elbow motion which is repeatedly performed in the 3rd form and can be used both as a block or a powerful close range strike.

Kwan Sao

Kwan Sao is a relatively complex rotating arm motion which can be used to block or roll out of a trap and is found in the dummy form.

Lan Sao

The Lan Sao or bar arm, is a lifting block. It looks similar to the Bong Sao but unlike the bong Sao the arm forearm is level with the shoulders and more or less parallel to the body and the rotation in the forearm is up not across.

Lap Sao

The Lap Sao is an interesting technique that destroys the balance and structure of an opponent, it has many uses most of which will be accompanied by a strike to deliver devastating force.

Lin Wan Kuen

Lim Wan Kuen or chain punching describes the rapid delivery of straight punches from the centerline.

Mann Sao

Mann Sao or inquisitive arm is used to gain contact with the opponent and can be used to block in a variety of ways.

Pak Sao

The Pak Sao or Slap Block is a simple yet effective block which is like many Wing Chun moves is the adaptation and refinement of a natural reflex to being attacked.

Pie Jarn

Pie Jarn is a horizontal hacking elbow strike that can be performed turning towards the target or away from the target. The power for it is developed in Chun Kiu

Po Pai Cheung

Po Pai is a complex double palm motion found in the Dummy form of the Wing Chun system, it can be used to strike, push or aggressively advance whilst maintaining positioning in the centre line.

Tan Sao

Tan Sao is an essential, common and yet effective Wing Chun block, this is found largely in the first form and dummy form.

Tok Sao

Tok Sao or lifting hand can be used to lift an opponents guard at the elbow in order to strike them or to throw them off balance.

Wu Sao

The Wu Sao or guard hand should always remain up when a hand is not in use as an extra failsafe cover. The Wu Sao should be in the perfect position to be launched forward as a block or strike.

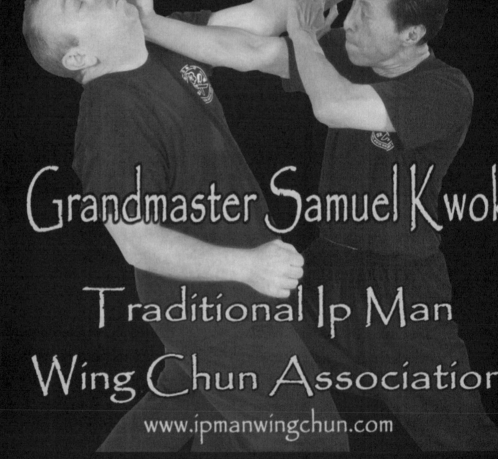

葉問詠春

Grandmaster Samuel Kwok

Traditional Ip Man

Wing Chun Association

www.ipmanwingchun.com

Those interested in knowing more about The Ip Man Wing Chun System, Master Kwok, and qualified instructors around the world can visit the web site of the

Traditional Ip Man Wing Chun Association
www.ipmanwingchun.com
or call **(757) 890-1188**

For products, equipment and information related to learning and training Wing Chun you can visit the
MASTERING WING CHUN web site
www.masteringwingchun.com

葉問詠春

葉問詠春

葉問詠春

葉問詠春